SEEDS OF TH

C000070539

SEEDS OF THE WORD

**Biblical Reflection
for Small Church Communities**

PETER B. PRICE

DARTON·LONGMAN + TODD

First published in 1996 by
Darton, Longman and Todd Ltd
1 Spencer Court
140–142 Wandsworth High Street
London SW18 4JJ

ISBN 0–232–52044–5

A catalogue record for this book is available from the British Library.

The Scripture quotations in this publication are taken
from *The New Jerusalem Bible* published and copyright 1985
and 1990 by Darton, Longman and Todd Ltd and Doubleday and Co. Inc.

Thanks are due to the following for permission to quote copyright
material: The Central Board of Finance of the Church of England for
*The Promise of His Glory – Services and Prayers for the Season from
All Saints to Candlemas* and for collects from *The Alternative Service
Book 1980* © The Central Board of Finance of the Church of England;
The United Society for the Propagation of the Gospel for *Let All The
World* edited by Wendy Robins and *A Still Place of Light* edited by
Robin Green. 'Come True Light' by Symeon is taken from *The SPCK
Book of Prayer*.

Illustrations are taken from *An Illuminated Version of 'Deer's Cry' or
'St Patrick Hymn'* by Archibald Knox. Used by kind permission of
The Manx Museum/Manx National Heritage.

Designed by Sandie Boccacci
Phototypeset in 10½/14 pt Times by Intype London Ltd
Printed and bound in Great Britain by
Redwood Books, Trowbridge, Wiltshire

For Jim, Guillermo, José, Carolee, Teo, Pat, Mark, Dee, Angela, Jeanne, Derek, and the many who are doing what the Word tells them and not just listening to it.

CONTENTS

PART 3: **Resourcing** *Seeds of the Word*

FOREWORD

In the darkest days of apartheid's worst repression, when we were becoming experts at conducting funerals because of the many victims of security force killings, we found the Bible to be a wonderful reservoir of sustaining words of comfort. Often and often the morale of our people would sag because the 'system', as the whole repressive apparatus of apartheid was known, was hellbent on knocking the stuffing out of them. It was rough: detentions without trial, states of emergency, mysterious deaths in detention, bannings, etc., were taking their toll and we had to try and lift our people's spirits. And the people were marvellous for their grit and resilience and extraordinary capacity to laugh, even at themselves, even at mass funerals after yet another massacre. It was as if the Bible had been written with our people and their plight in mind.

If the imperialists and others had meant to subjugate us and to keep us as perpetual hewers of wood and drawers of water, they should really not have given us the Bible, for it turned out to be the most revolutionary thing around. In a situation of injustice and oppression it was the most explosive, the most subversive instrument.

The Bible asserted that those who had their dignity trampled underfoot and who were treated like dirt as the victims of the awfulness of racist oppression, were creatures of infinite worth, a worth that was intrinsic to who they were and depended on nothing as extrinsic as skin colour. They were all this because they were created in God's image. They were God-carriers, sanctuaries of the Holy Spirit, indeed of the blessed and holy Trinity. Treating one of them as if they were less than this was a veritable blasphemy and was like spitting in God's face, for they were God's viceroys, God's stand-ins!

The Bible spoke about a God who was biased in favour of

the weak, the hungry, the unimportant, the marginalised, those who had no clout. God chose the side of a rabble of slaves against the might of the powerful and did so gratuitously, freely loving them before they deserved it or could earn being so chosen. This God intervened on behalf of a nonentity, Naboth, against the monarch. This God in Jesus Christ had solidarity with the unimportant ones, being born in a stable of parents who did not have enough clout even to squeeze a room from the innkeeper for a woman about to give birth. He kept disreputable company to the chagrin of the prim and proper ones. It was exhilarating to tell our people that our God heard their cry, saw their plight, knew their suffering and would come down to deliver us as he had done so spectacularly in the Exodus. You could sense the empowerment our people got from stories such as Elijah's contest with the prophets of Baal, when he taunted them and mockingly suggested they should shout louder because Baal might be deaf, or have gone on a journey and, insultingly, that Baal might have gone to relieve himself. We could say our God is not deaf, is not asleep, does not take a day off, but is always available for his people. It was exhilarating to use the story in Daniel of God delivering his servants from the fiery furnace, not by shouting good advice from a safe distance about the virtues of asbestos to protect from the ravages of fire, no, but by God actually coming down to be with his people in their anguish and suffering because this was indeed Immanuel, God with us. Their faith came alive on those occasions and their spirits were lifted because their God did not just have solidarity with them but had a veritable identification – 'In as much as you have done it to the least of these, you have done it to me'. Fantastic. And we could say using apocalyptic language that the victory of good over evil was assured, spectacularly proclaimed by the victory of Christ on the cross, demonstrated by the glorious resurrection.

Yes, the Bible was a source of very considerable comfort, strengthening us as if it had our condition and situation so very much in mind. I don't know whether the affluent and the

powerful and comfortable are able quite to understand the
Bible, whether their condition puts barriers between them and
the biblical perspectives. Jesus did say something about the
difficulty camels would experience in going through the eye of
a needle and the rich entering the Kingdom. Can you understand the logic of grace if you have reached the top largely
through your own efforts? Can you existentially understand
the absolute indispensability of grace?

Peter Price puts us in his debt by this 'how to' book on how
to unlock the wealth of the Scriptures in those splendid base
communities again discovered by people made desperate by
their circumstances of oppression and exploitation. I hope so
very much that our Church will grab the opportunity provided
by the increasing poverty of spirit, and of poverty in material
terms, in the West to make available the riches to be found in
the Bible. If they want to do this, no better guide is available
than this splendid book by Peter Price which I am happy and
honoured to recommend most warmly.

ARCHBISHOP DESMOND TUTU

PREFACE

'You know what's gone – you know, don't you?
Papa, Mama,' she said, 'and God, and the mystery of love.'
Her eyes filled.
    'All that's left is memory,' she said, 'and the memory's not
enough; the memory's one great longing.'[1]

I read these words on a visit to Tanzania in 1995. For me they
encapsulate the reason for writing this book. It is a poignant
reflection of our contemporary world, summing up the sense
of isolation and loss which many in our world face. In the so-
called 'Developing World' there is often a greater sense of
'God, and the mystery of love'. Their experience of loss is
often that of 'Papa, Mama' for through poverty, exploitation,
war, famine and conflict, many have lost their identity as
peoples, families, communities. In the West, it is not only a
reflection of those who have no sense of 'God, and the mystery
of love' in the formal religious sense – because it is also an
awareness experienced by many people within the life of the
institutional Church.

Seeds of the Word is a resource for people who are seeking
to rediscover hope in 'God and the mystery of love'. It seeks to
kindle a sense of belonging and community. It opens up the
Bible so that it can speak to the way things are where people
live. Through reflection, worship, prayer and discussion, *Seeds
of the Word* encourages people to engage in seeking transformation of their own lives, communities, environment and society.
It suggests that being church is more than belonging to a
Sunday congregation. *Seeds of the Word* is the product of being
part of a number of small church communities during the past
twenty years. It is also an expression of a longing to see such

faith communities become a model to wean us from the addictions of modern society.

Much of what is here has been tried and tested. Some of it began life as resource material for an International Partnership Consultation of Anglican Bishops, held at Whitelands College, Putney, in July 1990. Other material is drawn from programmes I have prepared, such as *Work with the Word* for the Adult Educators Conference at St Martin's College, Lancaster, as well as for *New Creation* in the Diocese of Southwark, and *New Way of being Church* at the College of the Ascension, Birmingham, and at Scargill. The majority of the reflections were written as *Seeds of the Word* in USPG's quarterly newspaper *TransMission*. It is partly in response to correspondence and support received from readers of *TransMission* that this book has been produced.

ACKNOWLEDGEMENTS

This book is the fruit of many encounters and the inspiration that they have given. Jim Wallis of Sojourners community in Washington and Mark Gornik of New Song in Baltimore have enabled me to see the call of God to both justice and community. My thanks to Guillermo Cook, now on the Evangelism desk of the World Council of Churches, for his encouragement to pursue biblical reflection from the perspective of the excluded; and to Fr Pat Clarke cssp and Sister Angela O'Toole, ss.cc for their example and insistence that I pay attention to the people on the edge, and who have drawn me into their own vision and vocation. I am grateful to José Marins, Carolee Chanona and Teo Trevisan, who have been my mentors in seeking to inculturate the experience of small Christian communities elsewhere in the world to Britain and Ireland; and to David L. Edwards, formerly Provost of Southwark Cathedral, for his unfailing enthusiasm for the freelance ministry he allowed me during my brief sojourn as residentiary canon.

I owe a particular debt of gratitude to my colleagues in USPG (The United Society for the Propagation of the Gospel), but especially to Jennifer Addie and Gill Macdonald for their unfailing patience, cheerfulness and fortitude in the face of increasingly unrealistic demands. Friends – Dilys Williams and Sylvia Roberts – and many others who have given helpful critical comments in reading the first draft.

I want to give special thanks to Daphne Jowit, who has prepared the manuscript for publication, not simply editing on the word-processor, but tidying up a thousand and one inconsistencies in the text, and advising on grammar, tense and style. Finally, I am indebted to Morag Reeve of Darton, Longman and Todd, for her patience, support and belief in the project.

PETER B. PRICE
Partnership House, All Souls Day 1995

PART 1

Preparing the Ground

1

. . . the seed is sprouting and growing.
(Mark 4:27)

A story
One Sunday I was invited to preach in a church on one of South London's sprawling housing estates. The congregation had no minister. When I arrived I was met by an overworked, disgruntled, and disillusioned lay worker. 'You do everything,' she told me curtly. There was no organist, or any other musical accompaniment, so I had to pitch a note for the hymns. Apart from a young black woman who acted as server and read the lesson, I 'did' everything. The congregation, numbering about twenty people, was scattered around the large church, with only a few sitting together in ones and twos.

The Gospel reading was from Luke 12 and included the words '. . . if the householder had known at what time the burglar would come, he would not have let anyone break through the wall of his house.' I looked around the scattered, dispirited congregation, and said, 'Yesterday my house was burgled and my family lost some things that were very precious to us.' I paused, then I found myself asking, 'Who here has been burgled?' Everyone's hand went up. I moved into the nave of the church, asking first one, and then another what had happened. Some spoke of what they had lost, others of how the robbers smashed the door, windows and even walls to get in. After a while, I asked if anyone could remember the Gospel reading. One or two did. I asked then if they knew of any other times when Jesus spoke about thieves and burglars. Someone remembered the words from John 10 where Jesus says, 'The thief comes only to steal and kill and destroy. I have come so that they might have life and have it to the full.'

We talked a little more about the shock and surprise that goes with being robbed at home, about the feelings of violation and the invasion of privacy. I then asked what would it mean 'to have life . . . to the full' in their neighbourhood. People replied that it would mean not being burgled or mugged, or fearing for their children. We discussed the need for people to be more alert and aware of one another. I asked who would be Jesus here? There was another pause, but then someone said, 'We should be Jesus here. We are the ones who worship God and say that makes a difference to people's lives.' I said, 'In the Gospel from Luke, Jesus said, "If he had known when the burglar was coming, the householder would have stayed awake." What does it mean for us to stay awake?' Someone replied, 'It means that we all share responsibility for making things different here.' Another said, 'We should be more caring, but we need to know each other better. We have to learn how to trust.'

And that's where the sermon ended. Except, at the sharing of the Peace, people smiled and moved around; as we gathered to celebrate the communion, the scattered congregation had formed into more of a group and moved nearer the front. After church we talked for a while, and people said they hoped that sermons in the future might turn into sharing their story, together with God's story – making an ongoing story in which change in the community could become possible.

The experience in South London that Sunday morning crystallised for me something about reading the Bible that has been a gradual change, a dawning realisation. It is a book of the people for the people, so that they can become the people of the Book. Most people only hear or read the Bible during the Sunday readings in church. Someone has described the way we listen to the Scripture readings as being like a habit – as smoking a cigarette is to a heavy smoker – when so many words are read they make little impact. People rarely listen to the Bible expecting it to make a difference to the way things are among the everyday realities of their life in the neighbour-hood or workplace.

In an attempt to encourage people to read the Bible more seriously, many churches plan Bible Study courses for seasons like Lent and Advent. While frequently enjoyed as occasions of increased fellowship, awareness and understanding, such groups seldom have any expectation of anything beyond the parameters of the season or the group meeting. In their every-day lives people are often aware of injustice, unfairness, dis-crimination, corruption and disregard for others, and while endeavouring to be personally honourable in their dealings with others, they feel they can make little significant change. People are not led to expect a change in the status quo. Most people believe that changing things is the prerogative of poli-ticians, church and other leaders. Few see themselves as agents of change, fewer still see the role of a church Bible study group significantly to affect the way things are, and to become a sign of hope.

Engaging the Gospel

This book is about engaging with the gospel. It is about *doing* as well as *being*. It will encourage people 'to do what the Word tells you and not just listen to it' (James 1:22). It is about reading the Bible from a different perspective. The congre-gation in that South London church had been used to hearing the Bible read and spoken about in sermons, but it rarely touched them where they were in their struggles on that estate. This is not meant as a criticism of either people or their minis-ters. Simply, neither had discovered the Bible as a tool for empowerment in the community.

The way we read the Bible is influenced by who we are, where we live, how we see ourselves, and how others see us. If we are middle-class, have a secure job and things we need to make life comfortable, those factors will influence the way we read the Bible. If, on the other hand, we are single parents, unemployed, living on inadequate benefits, housed in accom-

modation that is poorly maintained, or in a neighbourhood
that is hazardous to personal safety and ill-served by good
education, health and welfare services, then our reading of the
Bible will be different. As I have been privileged to meet
people in small church communities around the world, I am
struck that people who are excluded, poor, discriminated
against, easily identify with those, particularly in the Gospels,
who are like them. Middle-class people do not as easily identify
with their counterparts – particularly scribes, Pharisees, estate
managers, or even tax collectors!

Throughout the world, but in Western democracies in particular, the gap between rich and poor grows. As the gap
widens, there is a tendency among those who 'have' to gravitate
upwards, accepting the values of those who have power and
wealth, increasing their standard of living. Those, on the other
hand, who 'have not' drift towards increasing powerlessness,
loss of identity and dehumanisation. Most people have some
awareness of the injunction, 'love your neighbour as yourself,'
but the increasing width of the gap between rich and poor
creates tension and conflict.

This tension and conflict was illustrated for me by a young
woman, Ali, who during a discussion on her experience in
South Africa produced an elastic band. 'This represents the
tensions in my life,' she said. 'Ever since I returned from
Soweto, I knew I had to live in the inner city.' Together with
another woman, they had set up home in Birmingham, where
they shared their lives with the local people. 'Living in the
inner city challenges me at all sorts of levels. I have a good job
and a car. As I drove my car, I realised that I was closed off
from the homeless, unemployed people I lived among. I
decided to walk or catch the bus. When I stand in the post
office queue, I catch the sense of hopelessness of those waiting
to cash their giro, and I am challenged. For example, I can
go to a nice swimming pool. Or I can go where people who
live near me go, which is not so nice. When I was in South
Africa, I was not as challenged as I am now over racism, my

racism. There I was an outsider going in – racism was their problem. Now, I am having to face my own prejudices . . . and it is uncomfortable.'

Gospel for the Excluded

In many parts of the world in recent years there has been a growing realisation that Jesus had a particular concern for the excluded. In the Gospels the poor are the focus of Jesus' mission. Jesus lived in a society that was highly structured in favour of the 'haves'. Many were excluded to some extent – the mentally and physically ill, the maimed, certain professions (like shepherds, tanners, tax gatherers), as well as women, foreigners and children.

Each of the Gospel writers offers a perspective of who the excluded are in the eyes of Jesus. Luke speaks of 'the little ones', or 'those who cringe', in particular, women, children and others subject to discrimination like Samaritans, servants and the soldiers of the occupying power. Matthew, whose Gospel is written for an increasingly affluent church, reminds his members that they have a responsibility to re-order their resources in favour of the most needy. John sees poverty as powerlessness, he pictures people being disempowered by money, class, gender, race, education or by lack of political influence. Mark focuses on the crowds who follow Jesus. These have been described as 'the confused majority' and include such people as conscripted soldiers.[1] All these perspectives on the poor have one thing in common, namely that each category of people is in some way or another *excluded* from the ability to make significant life choices.

I write as someone who, like Ali, experiences the tension and conflict of being middle-class (white, male and a priest as well!) and who is confronted by the desire to ally with the powerful and influential, and yet at the same time knows deep within his heart that God is on the side of the excluded, 'the humble and meek' (Luke 1:52). In my travels, I find myself continually being converted by the witness of the excluded and

poor ones, evangelised by their faith, hope and humility. I
always feel I receive more than give. Being among the materially poor exposes my spiritual poverty. At the heart of this
kind of evangelism is a cry for justice that makes for a more
equal sharing of those things which enrich our humanity and
make hope possible. 'To know God is to do justice,' says a
Latin American theologian, Leonardo Boff. 'He defended the
cause of the poor and needy, and so all went well. Is that not
what it means to know me? says the Lord' (Jeremiah 22:16).

Remaking the Church
Seeds of the Word seeks to address this conflict and tension.
Most people in the Church in the West are middle-class. Most
have a spirit of generosity, a desire to live faithfully to the faith
tradition that calls people to 'love your neighbour as yourself'
(Mark 12:31). Often, unfortunately the spirit of the age calls
such people to selfishness, which leads to fence building and
excluding others. At the same time, something is happening to
many people in our affluent world which is both a threat and
an opportunity. All the accepted values of the middle-class are
under threat. Many of the securities of life, like full employ-
ment, secure home and family life, an agreed moral awareness
and a sense of community, are being knocked away. This pre-
viously *entitled* group, from whom the majority of church members come, once able to choose how to live their lives, find
themselves exposed to the fragility of life, where nothing is
certain. People in such circumstances feel themselves to be in
crisis. But times of crisis are both moments of danger and
opportunity.

An opportunity exists for remaking the Church in the affluent North. The challenge of the gospel is to be *inclusive*. Elsewhere the Church is being remade, becoming a place where
the *excluded*, the *little ones*, the *powerless*, the *confused majority*
feel at home. In countless thousands of small church communities, people are offering space so that 'simple people – the poor

who have been marginalised from both society and the church
– have a place where they can speak, be heard and discuss.'[2]

We need to begin where we are. The next two chapters give
guidance on group formation and using the resources in the
book. *Seeds of the Word* is based on the lectionary readings
for Year One in *The Alternative Service Book* published by the
Church of England in 1980. It starts on Advent Sunday and
finishes on the Fifth Sunday before Christmas the following
year. Don't let that put you off! It is not just for use by
Anglicans, but the author is Anglican, and believes that the
shape of the Church's year enables people to explore the
themes of the Christian faith, and the lectionary is a useful
tool.

This book encourages group formation with a view to transforming situations. It invites people to worship and pray
together. It calls them to reflect on the Bible, with a view to
acting on behalf of justice and the welfare of those who are
excluded. *Seeds of the Word* enables people not just to hear
and understand the gospel, but to *live* the gospel. In many
places around the world ' . . . the seed is sprouting and growing'
(Mark 4:27). Where people have little materially, new forms
and structures are emerging that make for ways of living that
build community and foster freedom.

A parable
*A woman and her children were emigrating from the country
into the city of São Paolo in Brazil. In the favela or shanty town
on the edge of town, she met a priest who worked there. She
asked him to help her find somewhere to live. He was kindly,
but could offer little help. A week or so later, the priest was
walking past a wooden shack, no bigger than a small living
room. The woman came rushing out, 'Come and see where I
live,' she urged him. Entering the 'house' he saw a row of
furniture lined up down the centre of the room. Wouldn't she
have more space, he suggested, if the furniture was around the
walls. 'You don't understand,' the woman explained, 'the man*

*and his wife whose house this is invited us to share it. They live
on one side of the room with their three children, and I live this
side with mine.' The priest remarked later, 'I couldn't do that. I
preach the gospel, but these people live it.'*

2

The seed is the word of God...
(Mark 4:14)

A story

In 1988 a group of people came together on an estate in South London. It was one of those soul-less concrete warrens of multi-storey flats, linked by enclosed, badly lit corridors. Few people attended the local churches on the periphery of the estate. Those who did saw themselves as 'survivors'. Under the inspiration of Roman Catholic sisters, a Methodist minister, and myself, a small group formed. The group stayed in existence on and off for nearly three years. The group was ecumenical, remnants of the Christian churches to which they belonged. The churches from which members came, though engaged in many good things, did not have the pastoral models and agenda to enable people to find hope in a situation where the physical environment was frequently both depressing and dangerous. 'Half the tenants here want to get out. All they want to do is to get off the estate,' said Louise to The Independent *newspaper in 1990.*

At the beginning of the group's life, when people told their stories, they concerned the fears of the group about burglary, violence and fear for their children. As we met, small red ants scurried across the floor among the group. In their own way they symbolised the oppression experienced by many in the neighbourhood. 'I opened a packet of biscuits yesterday,' said someone, 'and it was crawling with ants. Has anyone heard from the sanitation people?' No one had.

Although it took some time to establish, the group began reflecting on the Bible. The red ants found a ready parallel in the plagues that afflicted the people of God in the desert! Discussion on thieves breaking in and stealing, accounts of mugging, made reflection on the Good Samaritan very real. Hearing God's Word among such people is more than just the Bible. It is the **community**, *as well as the everyday* **reality**, *that enables it to be heard and spoken.*

The neighbourhood was always a focus for the group. The plague of red ants was a long saga, and little changed for a long time. The group drew up a petition and risked the hostile corridors and landings to get signatures. One or two people joined the group as a result of the campaign – though that was not the primary object. The local community association, itself poorly supported, saw the group as allies, and occasionally one of their members would come.

After a year the sanitation people came. Most people were out at work. Within the group just enough trust had grown up between some members for one to leave their key with another. Such trust building was slow in coming and quickly dashed. The group mirrored the neighbourhood. The **reality** *of everyday survival imposed itself each time the group planned to meet. Often people could not come to meetings. The reasons were clear enough, some arrived home from work late; there was no one to look after the children. Sickness, family, the vagaries of shift work, and the sheer physical weariness of it all, contributed to the difficulty of doing things regularly.*

Each time the group did meet, people shared something of their experience of life since the last meeting. Sometimes the story-telling went on all evening. People took turns hosting, organising, monitoring community action, being treasurer and recording the group memory. When someone had a birthday, got a job, passed an exam, or returned from visiting relatives or holiday, there was a simple celebration.

For such a group to meet once was something of an achievement. Meeting twice was a minor miracle, but to meet almost once every two weeks for nearly three years was a miracle indeed. Simple but profound acts of worship became part of the tradition too.

Groups for Faith and Action

We are living in times when people are looking for integrity in their faith. Many people in the Church feel a deep frustration with much that passes for church life. The experience of one Irish woman speaks for many: 'As a lay person, I have the impression that the official leaders of the Church often speak for me and sometimes at me, but rarely or never with me . . . If the official Church doesn't listen to the feelings of the people of God, it will lose the emotional allegiance of its members.'[1] Many people feel like this, even if they rarely articulate it. There is a resurgence of interest in community, in rediscovering a sense of belonging, and this is true within the established Churches and outside. There is a desire for a sense of belonging, in the search for a faith that sustains, supports and encourages participation in making the world a more hopeful and meaningful place.

Many groups in churches, or on the fringe of the church, meet together for discussion, prayer and action. Some groups are well established, others embryonic. Frequently groups are 'feeling' for a sense of direction, seeking some kind of consistency and the ability to be involved in action that makes for change. Such groups seek to go beyond just reading the Bible and praying, to become more aware of their place in the local community, neighbourhood, or workplace.

Seeds of the Word seeks to assist in this process of group formation. Some of the trial material has been used by neighbourhood groups on city estates, ecumenical groups, in preparation for confirmation, as the basis for church retreats, as a process of interaction between Advent or Lenten study groups and the ministry of the Word in the Sunday Eucharist. Although designed for group activity, many people have used the biblical reflections in their own devotions.

Many people meet in groups which resist any kind of structuring, either formal or informal. Groups like this occasionally function well, often they don't! Others meet in groups where everyone knows who is *the* leader. Sometimes these groups function well too, but more often than not such groups have 'voiceless' people in them, because the leadership is so strong that to disagree is pointless.

For several years now, the organisation for which I work has been facilitating a workshop at the College of the Ascension in Birmingham entitled *A New Way of being Church*. The programme encourages a method of group participation and leadership that has been borne out of the experience of many such groups around the world. For the most effective use of *Seeds of the Word*, I encourage those seeking to form small communities of faith, or those who are already part of one, to incorporate into your group life some, if not all, of the aspects of this model of group building and development. As a process, it makes for the greatest possible involvement of all participants, and leadership, though present in the group, is more effectively shared. At first glance, and even in early use, it may seem a little formal and over-structured – but experience has taught that it is worth persevering, because it works.

Things to Decide
Group forming requires the answer to some basic questions:

> Who wants to meet?
> Why do you want to meet?
> How often and for how long will you meet?
> Where will you meet?
> What will you do when you meet?

In answering those questions you will have begun to give some kind of shape to the group. It is often a good idea to plan an initial group-forming event in which there is some simple food, and opportunity for people to get to know each other better. Having some activity to help people to tell one another something of their story is good. A suggested exercise is the 'Tree Exercise'. It begins with people spending some time reflecting personally, and then suggests that people discuss together in groups of three or four.

Choose a Name

Groups often seek to find a **name**, in order to help create identity and a sense of belonging. For a while I belonged to a group called *One Step*: it symbolised how we felt about the tasks we faced in the neighbourhood 'one step at a time'. Often names come out of the process of story-telling. So as you share your stories, think of a name for the group.

The Tree of Life

(a) Ask each to think of a tree, the roots, trunk, branches, leaves, fruit, buds.

(b) Then ask each to think of their life as a tree in which:

Roots represent:	the family we come from, cultural background, strong influences which have shaped us, sources of life, vitality.
Trunk represents:	structure of our life today, job/work, home, organisation, communities, movements we belong to.
Branches represent:	the way our life has grown and changed,

	areas that have developed,
	what has been twisted, stunted or
	knotted,
	where a definite new direction has come,
	areas that have been cut off.
Leaves represent:	the process by which we get information
	and stimulation of ideas,
	people, media, newspapers, books,
	dreams, events, travel, reflection.
Fruits represent:	what we have achieved,
	family,
	projects,
	groups developed,
	materials produced,
	pioneer efforts.
Buds represent:	hopes for the future,
	dreams half-wished for,
	things just beginning.

(c) Each one reflects personally and draws their tree (25 mins.).

(d) Small groups of 3–4 people share their Tree of Life.[2]

Share ministries

In any group it is important to recognise the value of each member to the whole. To enable a group to function well, there are tasks, or **ministries**, in which each person should participate. The following suggestions for ministries are not exhaustive. The ministries outlined identify core tasks to be undertaken within a group to give it cohesion and structure. Everyone should share in ministry. These ministries may be rotated, and this is particularly necessary in larger groups, to ensure that no one is excluded. Some ministries are best done by more than one person, but these are matters for the group to decide. As the work of the group develops, so will new ministries, and the group should be alert to developing these as appropriate.

Welcome or *hospitality:* 'Welcome each other into your houses without grumbling' (1 Peter 4:9).

Making people feel welcome is essential for any group. Hospitality should always be simple, and not provide an occasion for

rivalry where people try to outdo each other. Those with the
ministry of welcome should seek to create an environment
where people can feel as comfortable as possible. While this
should not be elaborate, it is important to receive people in a
way that makes them feel accepted, and at the appropriate
time, bid them farewell.

Memory: 'Write the vision down . . . to be easily read'
(Habakkuk 2:2).
Groups need to be reminded of who they are, what they have
done, and what they have agreed to do. Group **memory** is the
key to effective change. It is a written reminder of what
the community has done and agreed. The **memory** should be
kept in a form where it can be passed on – a notebook or
loose-leaf folder is the best way. The memory should record
the activities and insights of the group, as well as keeping notes
of decisions taken, actions proposed and accomplished. The
memory is not the minutes of the group: it is a cross between
a history and a check-list. Whenever the group meets, the
memory should be shared. It can be acted out, read as a poem,
sung as a song, read verbatim – it matters not how it is done
– but *the memory must be remembered.*

Timekeeping: 'There is a time for every purpose under
heaven . . .' (Ecclesiastes 3:1).
Busy people need to know what they are committed to in terms
of time. All-too-many groups suffer from 'time-lag' because
they do not have an agreed start and finish. Because the groups
that you are forming have a number of activities, there needs
to be agreement about just how long each element of the
process can take. The **timekeeper** needs to work with the co-
ordinator of the group and agree this process. Early on in
group formation, people are often uneasy about this aspect of
the group but increasingly, as the tasks and vision of the fellowship develop, the proper allocation of time becomes essential.

Worship: 'God is spirit, and those who worship must worship in spirit and truth' (John 4:24).

Worship is at the heart of community life. Some simple act of worship should be part of each group meeting. The ministry of **worship co-ordination** is both a sensitive and self-effacing task. The worship of God gives focus to all our stories, reflection and activities. In each section of *Seeds of the Word* there are suggestions for worship.

News: 'This day is a day of good news' (2 Kings 7:9).

News is an increasingly important part of modern life. Whole networks of radio and television are given over to news gathering from around the world. The ministry of reading the **news** in the small group is essential for informing both prayer and action. Each meeting, items both serious and more light-hearted, that reflect the news of the week, should be presented. Once the group becomes involved in action in the community, the role and place of this ministry becomes increasingly significant. Once again, in the early stages, this ministry may seem a little artificial, but in time its relevance to the group and its work becomes both apparent and essential.

Celebration – fiesta!

The place of celebration – or as the Latin Americans have it *fiesta!* – is important in communities. Whenever the group gathers there should be some kind of celebration – a light-hearted moment. Birthdays and anniversaries provide occasions for merriment, but helping the group to celebrate simple achievements, or just have fun, is essential. In one sense no one can tell a group *how* to celebrate, or indeed *what* to celebrate. In each group someone needs to encourage and enable **celebration**. Don't be afraid of the occasional silliness or embarrassment, it too passes in favour of something genuinely celebratory as the group becomes more certain of itself.

Co-ordination: 'Make sure everything is done in a proper and orderly fashion' (1 Corinthians 14:40).

The group **co-ordinator** is responsible for drawing the various ministries together. The co-ordinator should not be seen as the group leader. His/her task is to ensure that the elements of welcome, memory, worship, timekeeping, news and celebration are incorporated into the group's life. The co-ordinator's responsibility is to enable the group to keep to its agreement to meet and hold the group to any tasks which it undertakes. It is a task that requires some skills at organising.

By practising these various **ministries** within the group, a sense of identity, a growing confidence, and an awareness of community grows.

The Role of *Seeds of the Word* in Small Community Formation

Small communities of believers around the world are discovering a fresh understanding of the **Bible** as a tool for everyday living. As people gather in **community**, they are finding the Bible both a necessary and contemporary resource in seeing how they can serve God better in the **reality** of everyday life in their neighbourhood, work-place, church and in the wider world. Hearing God's Word is not just a question of listening to the Bible being read, commented on, or even reading it. God's Word is heard when people read the Bible in the light of the everyday things that happen to them and other people in the situations in which they live and work.

Seeds of the Word attempts to encourage the use of the Bible as a tool for everyday living. By encouraging it to be read in the context of a small community, and by people who are having to face the realities of hope and despair in everyday life, it is hoped that people will 'hear God's Word' for our time. Or, as it has been illustrated:[3]

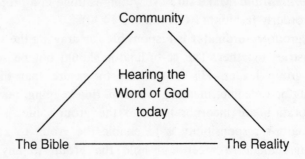

Or, to put it another way:

> One ear to the Word
> One ear to the world
> Speak a word of God for our time.

Getting Started

Each unit of *Seeds of the Word* begins with a *Getting started* suggestion. This, like the Tree Exercise, provides some kind of opportunity for personal history-giving, or story-telling. (You might like to glance through a few sessions to see what is meant.) *Getting started* provides a link to the theme of the week and often provides something of the **reality** the group members are facing day by day.

Bible

The **Bible** passage for each week is indicated by a simple instruction: e.g. *Read Luke 2:1–12*. As the Anglican *Alternative Service Book* Lectionary, from which the readings are taken, also has other readings set for the week, the instruction to *Read Luke 2:1–12*, will be followed by 'Other readings':

Read Luke 2:1–12.
(Other readings: Genesis 1:1–15; Colossians 3:1–10.)

The set reading is printed in the text, and is designed to be

read aloud. The version of the Bible used is the *New Jerusalem Bible*.

Comment

Each reading is followed by **Comment**. The Comment is a short reflection on the set reading. It is designed to be read aloud too, though it may help if everyone in the group has a copy of it to read for themselves. The ideas for Comment have been drawn from personal reflection and contemporary commentaries which have focused on how to live the Christian faith in our contemporary world. A full list appears in the Resource section at the end of the book.

Comment is designed to get you thinking, talking and acting. Each Comment is followed by **Talking Points**. The purpose of the questions or statements in Talking Points is simply to get you discussing together, hopefully reflecting on the Bible text, your own experience, as well as your neighbourhood or workplace.

Reflection and Action

Talking together is important, but so are **Reflection and Action**. Sometimes the Reflection will be a very personal response, but usually it is something the group should be doing together before deciding on some Action suggested by discussion and reflection. Each week time should be made in the group for reporting progress on any action taken – and of course it should be recorded in the memory. *Please note* that a more detailed description of **Reflection and Action** is included in chapter 3.

Worship

Each unit of *Seeds of the Word* contains either suggestions for a focus for **Worship** or a short act of worship. Occasionally *Getting started* suggests an act of worship together. Prayer is vital for groups who are going to engage in action of whatever kind. Worship is seen as an important and central activity within the life of the community group.

A parable

On my first visit to Brazil I spent time in the slums, the favelas or shanty towns of the big cities. In one such favela I went to visit the 'man of the brick house'. The house didn't look much, but alongside the wooden and tarpaulin shacks it was a mansion. The 'brick house man' was in his forties with a heart pacemaker. Every day he would pull his handcart around the city picking up a half brick here, a whole brick there. Filling his cart, he pulled it back and lodged the day's haul on the growing pile of bricks inside the 'walls' of his then wooden shack.

Day by painstaking day he collected the raw materials. Night by night he laid the bricks inside the wooden 'skin' of his house. He had a vision to build a house of bricks, first for himself, then another for his daughter. One day it was complete. The timber cladding came away, and the brick house was revealed. Today his daughter and the other members of his family have brick houses. He had a vision, you see. Every time he saw a discarded brick on the highway, he saw his house. For him the city streets held the promise of a home, among his neighbours, but different. A sign perhaps? A parable certainly.

3

Do what the Word tells you and don't just listen to it . . .

(James 1:22)

A story

Derek Hanscombe has for many years encouraged and trained young people, and helped them form small communities called Root Groups. *These communities of four or five people live, work and pray together in a local church situation for a year. During the 1980s much of the training took place in the East End of London. The 'rooties', as they were affectionately called, were encouraged to discover their neighbourhood. 'One of the local walks,' he remarks, 'was along a sewer bank – an endless vista of tower blocks, maisonettes, and industrial sites belching fumes. There was graffiti too, much of it quite beautiful. One year an exquisite Christmas picture appeared, with the words, "Happy Christmas to the East End". Another said, "No jobs, no money, no hope". Yet another showed a house wrapped in chains with the words, "Take care of your homes – if the Building Society doesn't get them, the Yuppies will." This was a passionate comment on the developing Docklands, which many saw as helping everyone except those who lived in the East End.'*

A Future under Construction

In South Africa recently my attention was drawn to some graffiti in a township, which read, 'The road to the future is always under construction'. When we look around our neighbourhood, or look at some of the problems our society faces, few of us can doubt the need for change. But if we want change, we must work and pray for change. Above all, we need to understand *what* has to be changed, and we need to discover *how* to assist the process of change. God both initiates in us the desire to make change and empowers us in the process. God invites our co-operation in the process of change which is already going on. All too often Christian people separate themselves off from the realities in which they live. Spirituality is seen as something 'other-worldly' rather than 'this-worldly'. The founder of the Iona Community, George Macleod, once remarked, 'there are few more dangerous words than *spiritual.*' The Iona Community has made its spirituality in the blood, sweat, toil and tears of life among the urban poor, as well as in peacemaking and concern for the environment. Yet this has been no well-meaning radical activism, but a self-giving, nurtured by prayer, biblical reflection and community, which have provided the power to engage with all that destroys abundant living.

Seeds of the Word sets out to encourage small communities to meet to pray, reflect on the Bible and to work for change in their neighbourhood or work-place. Jesus prayed, reflected and worked for change, which he described as 'God's saving justice' (Matthew 6:33). Justice here means *harmony or wholeness.* God's justice, or *kingdom*, or 'domination-free order',[1] is a vision of right relationships between people and God, people and their neighbours, and between people and the environment. Inviting his followers to join his mission of change, Jesus said, 'Set your hearts on his kingdom first, and on God's saving justice'. The writer Nikos Kazantzakis sums up the challenge of Jesus in these words, 'I believe in a world that does not exist, but by believing in it, I create. We call "non-existent" whatever we have not desired with sufficient strength.'[2]

Out of such vision hope is born. Hope, more than anything, is that which has empowered the Church in South Africa to engage in the struggle against apartheid, and now to be part of the new nation that is seeking to create a community of

justice and reconciliation at the heart of the modern world. A
T-shirt I saw recently had the following slogan painted on it,
'Hope is believing in spite of the evidence and watching the
evidence change'.

Reflection and Action
Look back at the story of the walk along the sewer bank. *What
was happening?* A community was being changed. Houses were
being built that were too expensive for local people; prices
were being forced up. Office blocks were being developed. Few
jobs came to local people, and many of the buildings were
surrounded by solid fencing, hiding and alienating at the same
time. *What was being said?* It was summed up in the graffiti,
'No money, no jobs, no hope'. As Paul Simon once wrote in a
song, 'the signs of the prophets are written on the subway
walls, the tenement halls . . .'[3]

In the **Reflection and Action** section of *Seeds of the Word*,
groups are encouraged to identify some situation in their neighbourhood or work-place which gives them cause for concern,
and which they would like to see changed. Before attempting
to act on things that cause concern, it is important to seek to
understand *why* things are the way they are. By asking the
question *why?* groups can begin some simple process of analysis, in order to get a more complete picture to see *how* it can
act most effectively.

Look at the following diagram which asks questions under
five headings:

Experience
Analysis
Reflection
Action
Celebration

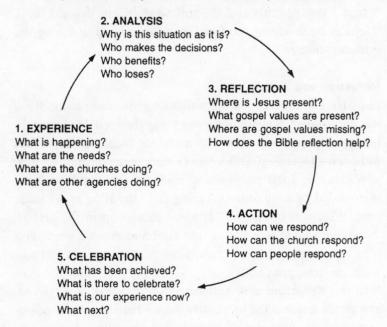

Experience, Analysis, Reflection, Action, Celebration

2. ANALYSIS
Why is this situation as it is?
Who makes the decisions?
Who benefits?
Who loses?

3. REFLECTION
Where is Jesus present?
What gospel values are present?
Where are gospel values missing?
How does the Bible reflection help?

1. EXPERIENCE
What is happening?
What are the needs?
What are the churches doing?
What are other agencies doing?

4. ACTION
How can we respond?
How can the church respond?
How can people respond?

5. CELEBRATION
What has been achieved?
What is there to celebrate?
What is our experience now?
What next?

Use this diagram, adding whatever questions you need whenever you do your **Reflection and Action** as a group. In church life, we are so unused to examining the things we do, and asking *why* we do them, that this process may seem a little strange at first, but once again it is worth persevering. Also, because we often do not know how to allow the Bible to influence our actions in the neighbourhood and work-place, we tend to relegate it to the pulpit, quiet personal meditation or the occasional Bible study group. Once again, taking biblical reflection seriously is often quite hard to begin with, but it is worth the struggle!

Finally, *be warned*! Whenever we tell our stories, or look at situations, we bring our values and our bias. As the author of this book, I may want you to think I am completely objective in everything I think, say, and do – but I am not, and neither are you! We need to recognise our bias whenever we want to be part of the process of changing things. We need to accept that we each have an agenda which influences our decisions. This book is biased! It takes as its starting-point the conviction that Jesus had a bias towards people who were excluded in some way, powerless, discriminated against, poor and confused; but they are the ones who are waiting for something to change. So *do what the Word tells you, and don't just listen to it.*

A parable

A young man asked his master, 'Where does the Messiah come from?' The master answered that he doesn't come from any-where. 'That's impossible. Everybody's somewhere.' The master replied, 'He's somewhere too. He's never been away.' 'Then where is he?' asked the young man. 'You'll find him among the beggars at the Gates of Rome.' 'But how can you tell it's him?' 'All the beggars,' said his master, 'have clean clothes to wear at the end of the day, and this is how they do it: they get undressed, go down to the river, wash their clothes, dry them and put them back on again. But not the Messiah. He removes one article of clothing at a time, washes it, dries it, puts it back on and begins the next one.' 'Why?' asked the young man. 'Because he wants to be ready to come at any time,' said his master. 'And when's that?' asked the young man. 'When enough people want him to,' the master answered.[4]

4

As for the seed in the rich soil, this is people with a
noble and generous heart who have heard the word
and take it to themselves and yield a harvest through
their perseverance.

(Luke 8:15)

A story
When the Gulf War started in 1991, we were living in Central
London. I felt such sadness and disappointment that once more
our country had to resort to war in order to establish a measure
of control over another country. I was aware that, as always is
the case with war, innocent civilians, women, men and children
would suffer and die in the midst of the conflict. One evening,
in very low spirits, I walked around the Georgian square where
we lived. I talked out loud to God and told him what I thought
about it all. I bargained with him and said that I, for my part,
would light a candle and pray every day if he would save the
life of one non combatant – man, woman or child of any
nationality or creed – by intervening in a way to ensure safety.
I felt good about the bargain I had struck, until it occurred to
me a few days later that I would probably never know if God
fulfilled his part of the bargain. However, this is where faith and
trust come in, and I was content.

I lit my candle every day. My neighbour, a politician's wife,
asked me why a candle was burning in my window and I told
her. She said she would do the same, so our candles burned
together on either side of our shared courtyard. Another neigh-
bour, whose husband had a very responsible job in the Ministry
of Defence, also asked me about it, she said she would pray, but
thought it best not to light a candle.

Shortly after, my husband went to a community group meeting in a very run-down block of flats, where he and some Catholic Sisters were working together with people to try to encourage faith, trust and a sense of well-being as a community in the midst of very difficult living circumstances. During that evening, one of the members of the group was rejoicing that her mother, who was away from the country visiting members of her family, had miraculously escaped a terrible disaster. She had been staying in an apartment building in Riyadh, Saudi Arabia. The apartments had been struck by the first 'Scud' missile to be launched at the city. Her mother and the other residents had all been out of the building at the time.

So, even in unlikely circumstances, God had encouraged me in that act of contemplation by letting me know that he had kept his side of the bargain.[1]

Praying for a Change

Prayer is often a last resort. This is particularly so for people who are activists. The subtlety of the temptation which believes 'one more big push' and the Powers will tumble, is very strong. But it is a lie, and later, if not sooner, the lie will be exposed and the ashes of superhuman efforts will be scattered once again on the floor of history. 'We are not easily reduced to prayer,' says Walter Wink. 'We who grope toward praying today are like a city gutted by fire. The struggle against injustice has exacted from us an awful cost.'[2]

We simply *have* to pray. Prayer provides hope when all our activity appears to lead to nothing. We do not have to pray according to any particular pattern. It may be symbolic, like the lighting of the candle in the window; or it may be a bargaining, like bartering in a bazaar. It may be a ranting, roaring type of prayer borne out of grief and anger; equally it may be essentially silence and contemplation. In and of itself prayer becomes its own protest, its cry against all that destroys humanity and creation and the work of God.

Prayer is more than protest: it is the place where God meets us. Prayer is the place where we discover hope. For when we pray we find a God already there, hoping like us for a future that is yet unmade. Prayer is the place where we discover a God who acts in history. Through prayer we can discern that we are not doomed to repeat the failures of the past.

Prayer then becomes the place in which we share with God in a hope for a future as yet unmade. In the Scriptures 'the question, "Who is God?" was answered with a reference to history – He is the God of Abraham, Isaac and Jacob. And the story of Jesus of Nazareth is part of that history, unintelligible without it.'³ An integral part of the struggle is discerning not only 'Who is God?' but 'Where is God?'

A group of people were gathering one Friday night in the hills above São Paolo for a weekend to study the Book of Revelation. As they gathered, they were singing in Portuguese, 'We are arriving'. As the song ended, the facilitator asked, 'Where are you "arriving" from? What are you coming for?' One woman, a nurse, was weeping. She had come from a hospital in the city. Day by day sacks of aborted foetuses were stacked outside the hospital. For her it was a haunting memory. 'Where is God?' she cried despairingly. There was a pause, and the facilitator, a priest, said, 'I don't know. Can we find him together?'

Even though the everyday realities of most of our lives are not as shocking as those of the nurse from São Paolo, most of us are seeking to find God in the everyday experiences of our lives. Finding God in the everyday is something we need to do together. We begin with the here-and-now things, what some-one has called the 'dailyness of life', and seek to discern or invoke God. So much of what we face is apparently inevitable that we hardly dare hope for real change. But prayer together calls us to both change and hope. 'It is better to light a candle than to curse the darkness' is a statement of hope and defiance. Prayer is learning how to defy the apparently inevitable, to turn from despair to hope. Prayer, or 'intercession is spiritual defiance of what is, in the name of what God has promised. Intercession visualises an alternative future to the one apparently fated by the momentum of current contradictory forces. It infuses the air of a time yet to be into the suffocating atmosphere of the present ... *History belongs to the intercessors, who believe the future into being.*[4]

Prayer as Untying God's Hands

For many of us, prayer is seen as something that we do in order to wake God up, in the hope we will get some action. We think *we* initiate prayer, *we* have noticed what's wrong with the world and, treating God like some kind of divine handyman, tell him to 'get things fixed'. Such a perception of prayer is mistaken to the point of being profoundly wrong. The reason we need to pray is that when we do not, our failure to pray somehow ties God's hands. His action is dependent on ours. The extent to which we pray determines how much we want to see the world change. How concerned are we like Abraham to see 'one righteous person saved' (Genesis 18) or, in the story above, witness through one person's prayer the saving of life among a whole block of flats hit by a missile?

Prayer as Listening to God's Prayers in Us

Prayer, or intercession, takes us into an act of co-creation with God. Whatever concern we have concerned God *before it concerned* us. St Paul says God is not only there before us, but actually forms for us the prayers that we seek to make – 'when we do not know how to pray properly, then the Spirit personally makes our petitions for us in groans that cannot be put into words' (Romans 8:26). God is so eager for change that we have only to *desire* to pray for change and God has already formed the prayer in us. Learning to listen to the voice of God within is something most of us find difficult. It involves an act of will and is marked by silence, rather than speech. 'We learn to pray,' says Wink, 'by stopping the attempt and simply *listening* to the prayer already being prayed in us.'[5]

In the **Worship** sections of *Seeds of the Word*, there is frequent use of silence, for it is only as we learn to listen that we

can discern what action we can and should take. 'We are not
called to do everything, to heal everything, to change everything, but only to do what God asks of us. And in the asking
is supplied the power to perform it.' When we understand and
practise this, a liberation takes place; firstly God's hands are
untied and joined to ours in an act of co-creation, and secondly
we are set free not to do everything, but to really do *something*.
We are able to accept a new prayer into our spirit: 'God, help
me to refuse ever to accept evil; by your Spirit empower me
to work for change precisely where and how you call me; and
free me from thinking I have to do everything.'

Prayer that Changes Us to Change the World

Marcel Moring's novel, *The Great Longing*, is a commentary
on the search for meaning in today's world. A particularly
poignant passage occurs when one of the characters comments:

> 'You know what's gone – you know, don't you? Papa,
> Mama,' she said, 'and God, and the mystery of love.'
> Her eyes filled.
> 'All that's left is memory,' she said, 'and the memory's
> not enough, the memory's one great longing.'[6]

Prayer is not just about achieving things: it is in essence the
process by which we encounter 'God and the mystery of love'.
Seeds of the Word encourages acts of worship within the frame-
work of growing as a community, biblical reflection and social
action. Worship is *more* than intercessory and listening prayer.
Worship seeks to give *worth-ship* to God, and to enable a spirit
of honour and yet enjoyment towards God. It is an act of
thanksgiving and praise in celebration of God's activity in the
world. Worship is the heart's response to God, it frequently
comes before understanding.

The decline of institutional religion and its frequent failure
to provide a spirituality for our times has meant that many
people have sought elsewhere for a sense of the numinous –
an experience of wonder, or of God. New Age religions have

sprung up offering psychological well-being, or forms of pan-
theism, the worship of nature, 'Mother Earth'. In Christian
terms, the decline of institutional religion has brought a fresh
examination of Celtic traditions, which paradoxically often
focus on the created order and our need to see and understand
God at work within it. The Orthodox Christian tradition has
captured the imagination of many who have sensed a loss of
awe and wonder in the worship offered in Western Christianity.

For many Christians, worship is a bit like a long-lost memory,
or 'one great longing'. We want something that will give us a
sense of God, both as present and presence. Contemporary
compilers of prayers often focus on God as loving, as creator,
but few capture a sense of the wholeness of God. Prayers are
too often centred on ourselves as human beings, few take us
to the heart of God. One of the early Christian mystics,
Symeon, called 'the New Theologian', strips away self-centred-
ness in prayer and offers a poem of worship which takes us
beyond ourselves into the very Being of God:

> Come, true light.
> Come, life eternal.
> Come, hidden mystery.
> Come, treasure without a name.
> Come, reality beyond words.
> Come, person beyond understanding.
> Come, rejoicing without end.
> Come, light that knows no evening.
> Come, unfailing expectation of the saved.
> Come, raising of the fallen.
> Come, resurrection of the dead.
> Come, all powerful, for unceasingly you create, refashion
> and change all things by your will alone.
> Come, invisible whom none may touch and handle.
> Come, for you continue always unmoved, yet at every
> instant you are wholly in movement; you draw near

to us who lie in hell, yet you remain higher than the
heavens.
Come, for your name fills our hearts with longing and is
ever on our lips; yet who you are and what your
nature is, we cannot say or know.
Come, Alone to the alone.
Come, for you are yourself the desire that is within me.
Come, the consolation of my humble soul.
Come, my joy, my endless delight.[7]

There is a search for the transcendent today. People are dissat-
isfied with the materialism and individualism of our contemporary world. But it is also more than that. There is a growing
sense among many who would not call themselves Christian
that there is something, or someone, greater than ourselves.
The French philosopher, André Malraux, counted himself an
agnostic, for atheism horrified him. Yet he was 'an unbeliever
so ardently in search of the transcendent that the world of
Christianity had become his own universe.'[8] Christianity
remains not so much rejected as untried, even by its closest
adherents. For many the teaching and example of Jesus point
to 'someone greater than ourselves', whose engagement and
concern for vulnerable humanity is both an inspiration and
example.

Robert Coles, in his studies of children and spirituality,
recounts a conversation between two eleven-year-olds, Norman
and Sylvia, whose brother Joey suffered from congenital cystic
fibrosis. They had been looking at Van Gogh's picture of *The
Wheatfield and Cypress Trees*. Sylvia had expressed her anger
about her brother's illness and questioned, ' "Does God know
all about this? – I'd like to know!" ' Norman responded,

'You've got to change the world, not just "settle for what
you've got." Maybe, if there's a God out there, that's the
one thing He's given us, that we can change things. There
are scientists; there are doctors; there's the space pro-

gramme; there's exploration in the oceans. I don't know
about God, whether He exists; but we're here, you, and
me and your brother, even if he's sick a lot, and we can
do something before we leave. I mean if your brother were
an artist, like Van Gogh, he could paint, even with cystic
fibrosis, and we'd appreciate him, like we do Van Gogh.
Even if he's not an artist, he can be what he is, he can be
your brother, and he's influencing you (isn't he?), just the
way Van Gogh influences us. It's complicated, all this, I
know. But you have to find something to believe in; you
can't just say it's all nothing out there. Like your own
brother says, there's beauty, there's the ocean, there's
waves and the sand, and the seashells, and there's people,
your parents, my folk, our friends: all that, and that's a *lot*
to "settle for".'[9]

Seeds of the Word seeks to encourage people to worship. It
recognises that people come from different places and experiences of life and faith. No one should feel excluded from the
worship offered in groups because they are still asking questions about God. The resources for worship are from 'the world
of Christianity', but are employed in such a way that members of groups can participate in worship from the space that
they occupy, rather than from one that is imposed. The group
experience of worship and prayer will bring its own changes,
its own revelations.

Seeds of the Word is a resource for those who believe, like
Norman, in Robert Coles' story, 'You've got to change the
world, and not "just settle for what you've got." ' Used sensi-
tively, there will be room in the groups that are formed for
many individuals, those who are sure of their faith perspective,
as well as those who are not. There will be space, too, for
others who are concerned to participate in making the world
a better place; who sense that if there is a God, his concern
must be for the most vulnerable, the excluded, the marginalised, the little ones and those who cringe. Call them what we

will, they are in any language or culture the beloved of God, and there is a place for them at the table of humanity which God seeks to lay with justice.

A parable

'In the night he was betrayed, Jesus took bread,' said the priest. Then he stopped, looked at the group around the kitchen table, and asked, 'Who here has been betrayed?' For nearly three-quarters of an hour, one by one the stories of betrayal poured out. When all seemed to have had their say, the priest commented, 'Now you know how it was for Jesus and Jesus knows how it is for you.' A little later he asked each person there to bring a symbol of their lives at present to the table. Some offered symbols that represented their anxiety, anger, sense of betrayal, and above all hope for the future. As the bread and wine were shared, one young man who interrupted the evening with his expletives and questions in almost equal measure, asked (expletive deleted!), 'Is this . . . religion?' 'What do you think?' asked the priest. 'I don't know,' replied the youth, 'but if it is, I'm coming back for more.'

5

Sow saving justice for yourselves,
reap a harvest of faithful love;
break up your fallow ground:
it is time to seek out the Lord
until he comes to rain saving justice down on you.

(Hosea 10:12)

Basic Preparation
This section is intended to help people every time they meet to form a group based on *Seeds of the Word*. Follow the guidelines carefully.

Becoming a group
Groups form in many ways. This book cannot tell you who to meet with, but it can offer you examples of different groups of people who have met using this material. Here are a few: a group of friends, neighbourhood groups working for social change, ecumenical groups during seasons like Lent and Advent, people preparing for baptism or confirmation, church retreats, groups meeting in order to interact with sermons during the Sunday service.

Having considered the kind of group you are seeking to form:

Decide
Why you are meeting;
who you are meeting with;
where you are meeting;
when you are going to meet.

At your first meeting:

Discuss:
How many sessions you are planning;
which *Seeds of the Word* units you will use;
how long each meeting will last;
what name you will choose for your group.

Organise ministries: Please reread pages 16–19.
Co-ordinator
Welcome
Memory
Timekeeping
Worship
News
Celebration
Remember it is important that each of these ministries is exercised whenever the group meets.

Planning Meetings

Each meeting begins with people being offered a **welcome** and some simple hospitality. This ministry, though natural to many people, is one which sets the tone for the whole group.

The **Co-ordinator** – makes sure people know **when** and **where** they are to meet.
– ensures that the other ministries of welcome, timekeeping, news, worship, memory (which is often helpful at the beginning of the meeting) and celebration are prepared.
– arranges for people to take responsibility for leading the group in:
Getting started
Bible reading
Talking Points
Reflection and Action.

During meetings, it is important that adequate **time** is given to the activities listed above. The **timekeeper** and **co-ordinator** should plan carefully and advise those with responsibility for leading the various elements of the meeting. Because the *Getting started* part of the meeting often involves personal history giving or worship, particular sensitivity in timing is essential.

Biblical Reflection

This part of the group meeting is very important, and again adequate time needs to be given to it. The following guidelines should be helpful:

- To begin, each person should *read* the passage for themselves.
- Someone should read the chosen passage aloud.
- Briefly share thoughts – has anything touched us personally?
- At this stage don't discuss – just allow the Scripture to connect.
- Someone should read the **Comment**.
- Where there are cross-references to other Bible passages, take time to see their relevance to the Comment.
- Allow a few minutes' discussion on the Comment.
- Discuss the **Talking Points**.
- At an appropriate time, move on to **Reflection and Action**.
- When indicated, either begin or conclude the meeting with **Worship**.

Memory – don't forget:

- To keep and share the group **memory**.
- To use the memory as the way for the group to monitor Reflection and Action.
- Do not lose sight of **celebration**
  - birthdays, anniversaries,
  - small (and great!) achievements in the group.
- Do make sure that there are copies of the Bible around.

Suggestions for **Worship** are offered in *Seeds of the Word*, and the **worship co-ordinator** should use these as the basis for the group's worship together. When the group decides how frequently it is going to meet, and where, it may be helpful to create some kind of group **focus** or altar, which symbolises both the season being observed and the group's concerns. A suggestion is offered at the beginning of each unit, as well as a reminder of the liturgical **colour** appropriate to the season. Colour has been associated with seasons and personal devotion as much for psychological as historical reasons. 'It seems natural, for instance, to associate red with blood, yellow with energy, white with purity, gold with festivity, purple with dignity, green with growth, light blue with hope, dark blue, violet and black with despair or mourning, and drab earth colours with burial.'[1]

Worship needs to be simple, yet creative. Using the resources and suggestions in *Seeds of the Word*, creating a focus, and being imaginative over the use of colour and light, an atmosphere can be created that encourages and empowers people to meditate and pray together.

And Finally!

This chapter has been designed to help you get the best not only from *Seeds of the Word*, but from the group life and commitment to the neighbourhood or work-place it encourages. However, these guidelines are not meant to tie or constrain you, and no doubt there are many better ways of doing things than have been suggested. You will find ways of doing things that suit your situation – and that's what matters. As I was closing this section, I read the following story from Anthony de Mello, which sums up all that I have just said:

A parable for religious educators:

> *A sheep found a hole in the fence*
> *and crept through it.*

He wandered far
and lost his way back.

Then he was being followed by a wolf.
He ran and ran, but the wolf kept
chasing him, until the shepherd came
and rescued him and carried him
lovingly back to the fold.

In spite of everyone's urgings
to the contrary, the shepherd refused
to nail up the hole in the
fence.[2]

PART 2

Seeds of the Word

ADVENT

Advent is a Latin word meaning *coming* or *arrival*. It is a time of expectation, of waiting for *someone* or *something* to come. The Church uses the term Advent to describe the period of time leading up to the celebration of the coming of Jesus Christ at Christmas. The *someone* who is coming is Jesus Christ – the *thing* that is coming is the outpoured love of God revealed in a person.

Advent is a time of preparation for Christmas. In many affluent parts of the world it is a busy, even hectic time, in which there is little opportunity to reflect on the coming of

Christ to the world. Advent is a time for repentance – becoming open to love. It is a time to prepare our hearts and minds to receive the outpoured love of God in Jesus Christ, so that we can share it anew with other people.

The themes for the four Sundays in Advent in *The Alternative Service Book* (ASB) are:

> *The Advent Hope*
> *The Word of God*
> *The Fore-runner*
> *The Annunciation*

Basic Preparation

As you begin *Seeds of the Word* for Advent, don't forget to reread pages 23–7. Agree **why, where** and **how** you are meeting; also decide on the allocation of **ministries**.

The Liturgical Colours for this season are **purple** or **violet, blue** and **black**. The colours for Christmas are **white** and **gold**.

Creating a Focus

The Advent ring, or wreath, has become a popular way of marking the season. Candles, greenery and seasonally coloured cloth can be used creatively to enhance the group's worship during this season.

Seasonal Collect:

> **Almighty God,**
> **give us grace to cast away the works of darkness**
> **and to put on the armour of light,**
> **now in the time of this mortal life,**
> **in which your Son Jesus Christ**
> **came to us in great humility:**
> **so that on the last day,**
> **when he shall come again in his glorious majesty**
> **to judge the living and the dead,**
> **we may rise to the life immortal;**

> **through him who is alive and reigns**
> **with you and the Holy Spirit,**
> **one God, now and for ever. Amen.**[1]

Note: Seeds of the Word is prepared for Advent, and for the Sundays in Epiphany onwards. The season of **Christmas** is not covered directly. Because most groups take a break during the festive season, the decision was made not to include Christmas studies.

First Week in Advent

Getting started

Do you have a favourite picture, either portrait or landscape? What do you most like about it? Why?

Read Luke 21:25–36.
(Other readings: Isaiah 52:7–10; 1 Thessalonians 5:1–11.)

25 'There will be signs in the sun and moon and stars; on earth nations in agony bewildered by the turmoil of the ocean and
26 its waves; men fainting away with terror and fear at what menaces the world, for the powers of heaven will be shaken.
27 And then they will see the Son of man coming in a cloud
28 with power and great glory. When these things begin to take place, stand erect, hold your heads high, because your liberation is near at hand.'

29   And he told them a parable, 'Look at the fig tree and
30 indeed every tree. As soon as you see them bud, you can see
31 for yourselves that summer is now near. So with you when you see these things happening: know that the kingdom of
32 God is near. In truth I tell you, before this generation has
33 passed away all will have taken place. Sky and earth will pass away, but my words will never pass away.

34   'Watch yourselves, or your hearts will be coarsened by debauchery and drunkenness and the cares of life, and that
35 day will come upon you unexpectedly, like a trap. For it will

come down on all those living on the face of the earth. Stay
36   awake, praying at all times for the strength to survive all that
is going to happen, and to hold your ground before the Son
of man.'

Comment

Luke, in this account, paints two pictures containing secrets
that are about to be revealed. The first picture provides great
drama – sun, moon, stars, all falling out of the sky! Each of
these symbols had meaning to Jesus' hearers: the stars represented tyranny; the sun and moon symbolised rulers and
empires. Each of the symbols represents powers that seek to
control human affairs.

Jesus told his followers to 'hold your heads high, because
your liberation is near at hand' (v. 28). The powers will be
shaken (v. 26). Jesus predicts that 'there are some standing
here who will not taste death' (Mark 9:1; Luke 21:32) until
they witness this event.

At the crucifixion, at the point of defeat, representatives of
the disciples, the women, Roman soldiers, Jewish authorities,
the powers, are witnesses to the end of the old order: 'There
was darkness over the whole land . . . and the veil of the Sanctuary was torn in two from top to bottom' (Mark 15:33, 38). The
Human One, the Son of Man, Jesus, triumphs.

The second picture is of a fig tree on a summer's day. Nothing
could be more idyllic and hopeful. The fig tree too is a symbol
representing peace, security and prosperity. The Jews believed
a fig tree in fruit was a sign of God's blessing. A good fig
symbolised a good person, or the people of God together acting
justly. 'Look at the fig tree,' says Jesus, 'see, the new order is
coming despite all that appears to the contrary.'

Talking Points

What do you think makes people good? Who would you
describe as good among the people you know? Who are the

people acting justly in the world today? In what ways are you as God's people acting to 'shake the powers' of injustice?

Action

Who is doing good in your neighbourhood? How are you helping? What else needs to be done? What could you as a group do?

Decide on what steps you will take. Who will do what? Report on progress next time you meet.

Worship

On page 238 there is a 'Liturgy for Advent' for you to use today.

For next week choose some people to prepare a short act of worship on *Good people.* You might like to have some readings from Martin Luther King, Desmond Tutu, Mother Teresa, Dorothy Day, or a saint.

Second Week in Advent

Getting started

Where do you feel most at home? What is your favourite place and time of day? Have you ever felt 'I don't belong here'? When, and where, was that feeling strongest? Why?

Read Isaiah 55.
(Other readings: 2 Timothy 3:14–4:5; John 5:36b–end.)

1   **Oh, come to the water all you who are thirsty;**
    though you have no money, come!
    Buy and eat; buy wine and milk
    without money, free!
2   **Why spend money on what cannot nourish**
    and your wages on what fails to satisfy?
    Listen carefully to me, and you will have good things to eat
    and rich food to enjoy.

3   Pay attention, come to me;
     listen, and you will live.
     I shall make an everlasting covenant with you
     in fulfilment of the favours promised to David.

4   Look, I have made him a witness to peoples,
     a leader and lawgiver to peoples.

5   Look, you will summon a nation unknown to you,
     a nation unknown to you will hurry to you
     for the sake of the Lord* your God,
     because the Holy One of Israel has glorified you.

6   Seek out the Lord while he is still to be found,
     call to him while he is still near.

7   Let the wicked abandon his way
     and the evil one his thoughts.
     Let him turn back to the Lord who will take pity on him,
     to our God, for he is rich in forgiveness;
     for my thoughts are not your thoughts

8   and your ways are not my ways,
     declares the Lord.

9   For the heavens are as high above earth
     as my ways are above your ways,
     my thoughts above your thoughts.

10   For, as the rain and the snow come down from the sky
     and do not return before having watered the earth,
     fertilising it and making it germinate
     to provide seed for the sower and food to eat,

11   so it is with the word that goes from my mouth:
     it will not return to me unfulfilled
     or before having carried out my good pleasure
     and having achieved what it was sent to do.

12   Yes, you will go out with joy
     and be led away in safety.

---

* The word translated 'the Lord' in this passage is 'Yahweh', the English form of
the Hebrew name for God, formed from the letters YHWH which is unpronounce-
able in English. The Hebrew people believed that they should not literally take
the name of God onto their lips without qualifying it.

> Mountains and hills will break into joyful cries before you
> and all the trees of the countryside clap their hands.

13 Cypress will grow instead of thorns,
> myrtle instead of nettles.
> And this will be fame for the Lord,
> an eternal monument never to be effaced.

Comment

Exile is a place or state of not belonging. It is a refusal to accept and conform to the prevailing culture and values. The people of Israel are in exile in Babylon and longing for home. Babylon is a symbol of the dominant powers which seek to destroy faith and community.

The dream of the exile is home. Home is the place where names are known; there is a place at the table, a sense of belonging, a place for sharing.

Isaiah is a poet who helps the exiles to dream. He reminds people of the joy and smell of buying fresh bread (Isaiah 55:1–2). In Babylon, the bread tastes stale. The poet says, 'Despite appearances things will change.' Speech is power. God speaks. God's word 'does not return empty, without succeeding in what it was sent to do' (v. 11). Imperial history will be changed, the exile will end, 'you will be led away to safety' (v. 12). It will seem as if creation has been transformed (vv. 12–13). Don't despair, says the poet, God's plans are different from those of the tyrants and rulers of empires (vv. 7–9).

'I have a dream', said Martin Luther King, and civil rights in America was born. Poets are subversives: they point to new possibilities of people living in harmony and community free from tyranny. Their poems don't change things, but the words they speak provide hope, energy, and the power to resist.

Talking Points

Who are the exiles in the world today? Are there any 'exiles' in your neighbourhood? What are their dreams? Who would

you describe as 'thirsty'? What is your church and group doing
for those 'who have no money'? What else could be done?

Reflection and Action
How did the action you took last week work out? How has
your discussion today helped you see what the next steps are?
What are the next steps? Decide what action to take, who will
do what and when? Report progress next week.

Worship
Offer your worship on *Good people*. Ask people to prepare
the worship for next time on the theme of *Hope*. You might
like to choose some Advent carols; also look for hopeful stories
in the newspapers; read one or two as part of your worship.

Third Week in Advent

Getting started
What makes you hopeful? Do you have a particular hope for
yourself that you would like to see fulfilled one day? What is it?

Read Isaiah 40:1–11.
(Other readings: 1 Corinthians 4:1–5; John 1:19–28.)

1   **'Console my people, console them,'**
     says your God.
2   **'Speak to the heart of Jerusalem**
     and cry to her
     that her period of service is ended,
     that her guilt has been atoned for,
     that, from the hand of the Lord, she has received
     double punishment for all her sins.'
3   **A voice cries, 'Prepare in the desert**
     a way for the Lord.
     Make a straight highway for our God
     across the wastelands.

4   Let every valley be filled in,
    every mountain and hill be levelled,
    every cliff become a plateau,
    every escarpment a plain;
5   then the glory of the Lord will be revealed
    and all humanity will see it together
    for the mouth of the Lord has spoken.'
6   A voice said, 'Cry aloud!' and I said, 'What shall I cry?'
    – 'All humanity is grass
    and all its beauty like the wild flower's.
7   The grass withers, the flower fades
    when the breath of the Lord blows on them.
    (The grass is surely the people.)
8   The grass withers, the flower fades,
    but the word of our God remains for ever.'
9   Go up on a high mountain,
    messenger of Zion.
    Shout as loud as you can,
    messenger of Jerusalem!
    Shout fearlessly,
    say to the towns of Judah,
    'Here is your God.'
10 Here is the Lord God coming with power,
    his arm maintains his authority,
    his reward is with him
    and his prize precedes him.
11 He is like a shepherd feeding his flock,
    gathering lambs in his arms,
    holding them against his breast
    and leading to their rest the mother ewes.

Comment

Anger, depression, guilt and powerlessness are the experience
of people in exile or prison. Past actions trap people in despair.
The subversive poet sees the danger of despair and knows his
poetry must nurture, inspire and empower change. He speaks

words of comfort (v. 1) and forgiveness (v. 2). Hope is generated.

For God's people a new plan in history is in the making (vv. 3–4). It will be a public event – 'all humanity will see it together' (v. 5). People once afraid now speak. Fear has been overcome. God's apparent powerlessness during the exile has been transformed into a God reclaiming sovereignty: 'Here is your God' (vv. 9–10).

Now is the time for action: the exiles must embrace faith in God, discern their true political situation, and choose to act. 'Prepare . . . Make a straight way . . . for God' (vv. 3,9). The overriding power of God's word will have its say in history (Isaiah 40:6–8; 55:10–11). In one sense nothing has changed, and yet at the same time everything has changed. Despair has been overcome, people are singing (Isaiah 52:7). Through the years of suffering and grief comfort has come, forgiveness is experienced, and hopes raised of a home-coming.

Talking Points
Have you any experience of anger, depression or guilt? What made you that way? How did things change? Who in your neighbourhood needs comfort? What past actions in your church and community need putting right? What is forgiveness? How can forgiveness be brought into the concerns you have about your neighbourhood?

Reflection and Action
Report on progress since your last meeting.

Has today's study helped you think about the next, or new, steps in fulfilling your chosen task? Are your goals still clear? Do you need more information, help, re-evaluation? What's next?

Check page 26 to see that you are asking the right questions.

Worship

Offer your worship on *Hope*.

Prepare for next week: choose some carols that speak to you of the hope for justice and peace in our world.

Celebration

Next week marks the conclusion of Advent. Plan a celebration of your time together. The Christmas season provides many options to consider: you could have 'punch and mince pies' or a simple shared meal where everyone brings a dish; or you could go carol singing – be imaginative and creative. But do celebrate!

Fourth Week in Advent

Getting started

This week marks the conclusion of the Advent *Seeds of the Word*. What has been important to you about these times of meeting? In what ways has it been different from anything you have done before? Choose one word that sums up the experience for you.

Read Luke 1:26–38.
(Other readings: Isaiah 11:1–9; 1 Corinthians 1:26–end.)

26 In the sixth month the angel Gabriel was sent by God to a
27 town in Galilee called Nazareth, to a virgin betrothed to
    a man named Joseph, of the House of David; and the virgin's
28 name was Mary. He went in and said to her, 'Rejoice, you
29 who enjoy God's favour! The Lord is with you.' She was
    deeply disturbed by these words and asked herself what this
30 greeting could mean, but the angel said to her, 'Mary, do not
31 be afraid; you have won God's favour. Look! You are to
    conceive in your womb and bear a son, and you must name
32 him Jesus. He will be great and will be called Son of the
    Most High. The Lord God will give him the throne of his

33   ancestor David; he will rule over the House of Jacob for ever
34   and his reign will have no end.' Mary said to the angel, 'But
      how can this come about, since I have no knowledge of man?'
35   The angel answered, 'The Holy Spirit will come upon you,
      and the power of the Most High will cover you with its
      shadow. And so the child will be holy, and will be called Son
36   of God. And I tell you this too: your cousin Elizabeth also,
      in her old age, has conceived a son, and she whom people
37   called barren is now in her sixth month for nothing is imposs-
38   ible to God. Mary said, 'You see before you the Lord's ser-
      vant, let it happen to me as you have said.' And the angel
      left her.

Comment

The impossible is possible (v. 37). A barren woman becomes
pregnant (v. 36). A virgin conceives (v. 35). Angels speak, and
the messenger Gabriel tells Mary, 'You shall call the child
Jesus' (or Joshua) – the name of a freedom fighter. Mary is
told, too, that her son shall assume 'the throne of his ancestor
David' (vv. 32–3). His rule will be marked by the eternal
qualities of justice and righteousness (Psalm 89:14). The angel
offers a strongly political message, that Jesus will fulfil (vv.
32–4) the hopes and dreams of generations who have longed
for liberation.

Overwhelmed by the expectations of her as yet unconceived
child, Mary humbly asks, 'How can this be, since I have no
husband?' (v. 34) Suddenly everything has become very human.
God chooses to achieve his purpose in simple and surprising
places: a person's will, a mother's womb, a displaced birth
(Luke 2:4–5), life among the outcast and the poor (Matthew
8:20; Luke 7:34). In the child of the barren one, the moment
of 'quickening' becomes the sign of God's Spirit being received
into another human being (v. 41).

When women like Elizabeth and Mary find the courage to
co-operate with God, the impossible becomes possible. Mary's
trusting openness to love gave birth to Love in the world.

Impossible though it seems, today the same power and love can be liberated through people in this age too. Elizabeth could not but express continued surprise, 'Why should I be honoured with a visit from the mother of my Lord?' (v. 43) There is no answer as to why God should visit anyone – it is a gift, and it is called grace. Like the wife of Zechariah, and the betrothed to Joseph, all that is required to receive the gift is the belief 'nothing is impossible for God' (v. 37).

Talking Points

Have you ever experienced the impossible becoming possible? What happened? Have you ever seen love coming to birth as a result of someone's courage and openness? What is the most courageous thing you have ever done? How have the past few weeks strengthened your courage and made you more open to others?

Reflection and Action

Review the action you have taken during the past few weeks as a group, or an individual, to bring about some change in a local situation. Reflect on what happened. What did you do? In what ways will you be more available to others this Christmas? What plans have you to meet together again as a group? When? Why?

Worship and Celebration

Offer your worship of carols with themes of *Justice* and *Peace*. Follow it with the celebration that you have planned of your life together.

EPIPHANY

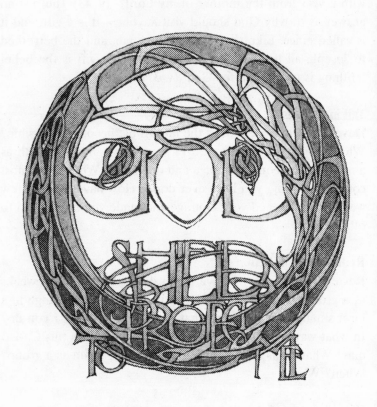

The word **epiphany** means to 'reveal' or to 'manifest'. The Christian feast of the **Epiphany** is a celebration of God being revealed and becoming known in the person of Jesus Christ. The Church has traditionally seen this as a season in which to seek to understand who God is for us. The Feast of the Epiphany begins on 6 January with the **revealing** of God to the Wise Men, or Magi. Epiphany is also about God being revealed through the baptism of Jesus. Epiphany is a season for allowing our minds and hearts to be open to seeing God.

The themes for the six Sundays in Epiphany in *The Alternative Service Book* are:

The Baptism of Jesus
The First Disciples
Signs of Glory
The New Temple
The Wisdom of God
Parables

The themes of Epiphany are grouped under the general title **Revelation**. 'Revelation' is the Word of God making himself known in historical acts. The question 'Who is God?' was answered with reference to history – this is the God of Abraham, Isaac and Jacob. And the story of Jesus of Nazareth is part of that history and unintelligible without it.[1]

Basic Preparation
As you begin *Seeds of the Word* for Epiphany, don't forget to reread pages 23–7. Agree **why, where** and **how** you are meeting; also decide on the allocation of **ministries**.
   The Liturgical Colours are **white, gold** and **green**.

Creating a Focus
The festival colours of white and gold symbolise both what is pure and precious. White also symbolises baptism. For this seasonal focus members of the group could bring something that symbolises the value of their baptism and life of faith.

Seasonal Collect:

Eternal God,
who by the shining of a star
led the wise men to the worship of your Son:
guide by his light the nations of the earth,
that the whole world may behold your glory;
through Jesus Christ our Lord. AMEN.[2]

Note: The calendar rarely provides opportunity for all six Sundays in Epiphany to be observed. *Seeds of the Word* includes all six because there is a sense of completeness to the themes. You may wish to use only some of them before moving into the Sundays before Easter, or you may choose to persist with all six leaving out the reflections on the **Ninth, Eighth and Seventh Sundays before Easter.**

First Sunday in Epiphany

Getting started
Ask each person in the group to share when in their personal history the question 'Who is God for me?' began to be answered.

Read Matthew 3:13–end.
(Other readings: 1 Samuel 16:1–13a; Acts 10:24–38.)

13 **Then Jesus appeared: he came from Galilee to the Jordan to**
14 **be baptised by John. John tried to dissuade him, with the**
    words, 'It is I who need baptism from you, and yet you come
15 **to me!' But Jesus replied, 'Leave it like this for the time**
    being; it is fitting that we should, in this way, do all that
    uprightness demands.' Then John gave in to him.
16 **And when Jesus had been baptised he at once came up**
    from the water, and suddenly the heavens opened and he saw
    the Spirit of God descending like a dove and coming down
17 **on him. And suddenly there was a voice from heaven, 'This**
    is my Son, the Beloved; my favour rests on him.'

Comment
'Jesus arrived . . . from Galilee' (v. 13). (It was a notorious region to the religious authorities in Jerusalem.) A poor province, populated by non-Jews, separated from 'true Israel' by another notorious area, Samaria, Galilee was a hiding place for guerrillas, and a hotbed of revolution. We should be warned! If Jesus comes from here – he is identified as potential trouble!

He comes to be baptised and stands in line with thousands of others. John, his cousin, Elizabeth's son, has been urging baptism on others (3:1–12), but now he is reticent, because he recognises God's chosen one (v. 14). 'It is fitting ... [to] do all that uprightness demands', Jesus tells John.

What can he mean? Did Jesus need to repent too? Unless the gesture is an empty one, apparently he did. John had been announcing a coming new order; his baptism prepared people for new ways of living and behaving. Jesus provides the focus of the new order. His baptism was a sign of renouncing the old order; his act of repentance gave a signal that he was making a break with structures and values in society by which people are oppressed. He was signalling an end to his involvement with the prevailing moral and religious order.

Two dramatic events follow the baptism of Jesus: the alighting of a dove and the voice of God (v. 16). Both these signs confirm for Jesus the rightness of his action. He will need all the courage and faith he can get as he faces the conflict, drama, and temptation to give up his calling in the desert (4:1–11).

Talking Points
'Attention! Don't baptise your child if you don't know what baptism is about! He can get into hot water ... Whoever accompanies Jesus and lives like he lived is going to get into hot water like he did ...' These words are part of a re-evangelization programme among poor Catholics in Brazil. What is our understanding of baptism? Does either the Comment or the above story give us any new insights? How does your church understand and practise baptism today?

Reflection and Action
Review your understanding of baptism. Find your baptism certificate; look at the date of your baptism, where it was held, who your godparents are. Bring your certificate to your next meeting. Are you a godparent? What does that mean for you?

Worship
Use the Liturgy for Reconciliation on page 239.

For next week, bring a candle to symbolise your baptism. As an act of recommitment and repentance, use some of the readings and prayers in the Alternative Service Baptism service, or a similar rite from another denomination.

Second Sunday in Epiphany

Getting started
Ask each person to share their baptism certificate. Talk about the date and place of baptism, and who the godparents were. Light the candles and share significant moments of your faith journey since your baptism. Offer the readings and prayers suggested last week as an act of commitment and repentance.

Read Mark 1:14–20.
(Other readings: Jeremiah 1:4–10; Acts 26:1,9–20.)

14 **After John had been arrested, Jesus went into Galilee. There**
15 **he proclaimed the gospel from God saying, 'The time is fulfilled, and the kingdom of God is close at hand. Repent, and believe the gospel.'**
16 **As he was walking along by the lake of Galilee, he saw Simon and Simon's brother Andrew casting a net in the lake**
17 **– for they were fishermen. And Jesus said to them, 'Come**
18 **after me and I will make you into fishers of people.' And at once they left their nets and followed him.**
19 **Going on a little further, he saw James son of Zebedee and his brother John; they too were in their boat, mending the**
20 **nets. At once he called them, and leaving their father Zebedee in the boat with the men he employed, they went after him.**

Comment
'After John had been arrested ... Jesus came ... proclaiming ... "the time has come" ' (vv. 14–15). John's arrest as

a subversive is followed by Jesus demonstrating his solidarity and identity with him by taking up his message. The assault on the old order has begun: 'Repent and believe the gospel', declares Jesus. The strategy opens by forming a discipleship community; their distinct task is to be 'fishers of people' (v. 18). In the Old Testament 'hooking fish' is a phrase used by the prophets to imply judgement on the rich and powerful (Amos 4:2; Ezekiel 29:4). The fishermen are to join in the struggle against the powerful and privileged who oppress the poor and weak.

Most fishermen were small, independent, often family businessmen who could afford 'hired men' (v. 20), to whom they could leave their work when at market or making business contracts. The fishermen who 'leave their nets and follow' are also offered an invitation to repentance. Jesus challenges them to make the break with social and economic security for a few, for the sake of all. To follow Jesus, then, is to break with 'business as usual', and grasp the opportunity to become disciples, learning to build a new social order.

Mark is the first writer to use the term 'gospel'. A gospel was a secular Roman propaganda sheet designed to get obedience from the local peasantry, and loyalty to the emperor. By stealing this term, Mark wants to emphasise a new ruler and a new rule – 'the kingdom of God is close at hand' (v. 14).

Talking Points

How do you react to the idea that Jesus invited people to join the struggle against the powerful and privileged?

Would-be disciples usually sought their teacher, or rabbi. Jesus, on the other hand, sought and found his disciples. What does this say to you about the kind of discipleship Jesus invites? Which people of faith do you admire and seek to follow in some way? Why?

Reflection and Action
Discipleship is like a school course for which there is no final exam! It is a continual assessment on the question of 'How are you understanding and practising the gospel of God?' So, what new understanding have you gained into the gospel in the past few weeks? How are you putting it into practice? What would it mean in your situation to respond to the invitation of Jesus to become 'fishers of people'?

Discuss a strategy for action.

Worship
For next week gather articles from newspapers or magazines which provide examples of how the existing order has in some way been turned upside-down. Each person should write a short prayer *or* choose a verse or two from the Bible which speaks about such a situation.

Third Sunday in Epiphany

Getting started
Begin with an act of worship, in which you offer the signs of the existing order being changed, that you chose during the past week.

Read John 2:1–11.
(Other readings: Exodus 33:12–end; 1 John 1:1–7.)

1 **On the third day there was a wedding at Cana in Galilee.**
2 **The mother of Jesus was there, and Jesus and his disciples**
3 **had also been invited. And they ran out of wine, since the wine provided for the feast had all been used, and the mother**
4 **of Jesus said to him, 'They have no wine.' Jesus said, 'Woman,**
5 **what do you want from me? My hour has not come yet.' His**
6 **mother said to the servants, 'Do whatever he tells you.' There were six stone water jars standing there, meant for the ablutions that are customary among the Jews: each could**
7 **hold twenty or thirty gallons. Jesus said to the servants, 'Fill**

8   the jars with water,' and they filled them to the brim. Then
he said to them, 'Draw some out now and take it to the
9   president of the feast.' They did this; the president tasted
the water, and it had turned into wine. Having no idea where
it came from – though the servants who had drawn the water
10   knew – the president of the feast called the bridegroom and
said, 'Everyone serves good wine first and the worse wine
when the guests are well wined; but you have kept the best
wine till now.'
11   This was the first of Jesus' signs: it was at Cana in Galilee.
He revealed his glory and his disciples believed in him.

Comment

In the everyday-ness of life it is hard to see things getting better.
'The poor are always with you', said Jesus on one occasion. The
Gospel writers understood this reality too. John tells about the
signs of power and the actions which Jesus did, like the turning
of water into wine in Cana. These signs always invite a
response of belief, not only in Jesus, but in the power of God
to bring life-giving, life-enhancing and life-saving change to all
people.

Jesus' apparent rudeness to his mother is shocking – he says,
in effect, 'mind your own business' (v. 4). In light of the tightly-
knit family dynamics of the biblical world, Jesus' apparent
disregard for his mother's honour/shame is shocking.[3] No
special privilege is offered to blood relationships in the new
order.

In many ways the changing of the water into wine seems a
frivolous sign – albeit an enjoyable one. Certainly the president
of the feast can only make a somewhat ironic remark (v. 10).
Perhaps the key to understanding it lies in the trust it engen-
dered in Jesus' disciples (v. 11).

John implies that Jesus' actions are of his own choosing, and
when change happens as a result, it can be dramatic. In the
complex and often insuperable problems of our world today
we need John's view of Jesus to remind us that God acts in

history. When human beings make acts of resistance and trust, in order to bring hope and life to others, they share in God's actions.

The president of a banquet was someone of status. People with status were thought to be 'in the know'. On this occasion, the servants who 'had drawn the water knew' while the president had 'no idea' (v. 9) where the wine came from. Often it is those nearest to the realities of everyday life, and yet are the most excluded from power, who discern God at work in those human beings who seek change that is life-enhancing, and life-saving.

Talking Points

Where are the signs of God's activity in history that give you cause for encouragement and hope? From the news stories you have identified this week are there people, or things happening, that make you wonder if God is acting specifically in situations? If not, what do you think it would take? What areas of life could be changed if only others would join you in helping to change them?

Reflection and Action

What do you have to report following the action you decided on last week in seeking to become 'fishers of people'? In the light of your worship, reading and discussion today, can you identify small places where you as a group can influence and make change?

Worship

In your preparation for worship next time, bring something to the group which is valuable to you, and share its significance. What would it mean to you if you lost it? As you become aware of events in the world this week, reflect on those news stories in which people lose something or everything.

Fourth Sunday in Epiphany

Getting started

Begin by sharing the things of value that you have each brought. Say why they are valuable to you. What would it mean to each of you if you lost this item? What event in the news were you aware of in which people lost everything? Offer prayers of thanksgiving for the treasures in your life. Pray for those who this week have lost everything.

Read 1 Corinthians 3:10–17.
(Other readings: 1 Kings 8:22–30; John 2:13–22.)

10 By the grace of God which was given to me, I laid the foundations like a trained master-builder, and someone else is building on them. Now each must be careful how he does

11 the building. For nobody can lay down any other foundation

12 than the one which is there already, namely Jesus Christ. On this foundation different people may build in gold, silver,

13 jewels, wood, hay or straw, but each person's handiwork will be shown for what it is. The Day which dawns in fire will make it clear and the fire itself will test the quality of each person's

14 work. The one whose work stands up to it will be given his

15 wages; the one whose work is burnt down will suffer the loss of it, though he himself will be saved; he will be saved as someone might expect to be saved from a fire.

16   Do you not realise that you are a temple of God with the

17 Spirit of God living in you? If anybody should destroy the temple of God, God will destroy that person, because God's temple is holy; and you are that temple.

Comment

Foundations need to be properly constructed if a building is to stand. St Paul prided himself on building faith communities among people who were on the margins. Like Jesus, he believed that 'God chose those who by human standards . . . count for nothing' (1 Corinthians 1:27–8). Paul made it his 'rule to preach

the gospel only where the name of Christ has not already been
heard, for I do not build on another's foundations' (Romans
15:20).

In Paul's communities living a new way of life was more
important than learning new doctrines. Keeping the faith is
always as much about how people live as it is about what they
believe. The faith Paul taught was understood by farm workers
(v. 9), wage earners (v. 14) and the 'common and contemptible'
(1 Corinthians 1:28). In practice, this meant seeing God in the
small everyday things of life, 'Whatever you eat, then, or drink,
and whatever else you do, do it all for the glory of God' (1
Corinthians 10:31).

The most valuable foundations of community building, 'the
gold, silver, jewels' (v. 12), are in refusing to attract attention
to oneself (Luke 14:7–10; Mark 10:45; Romans 12:10); being
sincere (Matthew 5:37); being discreet and knowing when to
speak and to be silent (James 3:3–10; Matthew 18:15); avoiding
anxiety and preoccupation with the future (Matthew 6:32–4);
being pleasant (Matthew 6:16) and always wanting to do good
(Romans 12:51); being on time (Matthew 25:1–13); avoiding
laziness and inactivity (Matthew 20:1–16); persevering and
sticking with the faith through thick and thin (Luke 9:62;
Matthew 24:13; 25:21). Such familiar and everyday things were
important in the household community churches. Living out
these 'little virtues' of hearth and home – actually very demanding virtues – corresponds to the original intentions of Jesus of
Nazareth, who sought to heal living interpersonal relationships
from *'within the community'*.[4]

The temple of God is no longer a sacred building, but a
community of people, made up of individual members. By
the day-by-day practice of 'little virtues', they are presenting
themselves as 'living sacrifices to God', (Romans 12:1) and
building their lives on the foundation 'which is already there,
namely Jesus Christ.'

Talking Points

Do you agree that the 'little virtues' are in fact very demanding? What place do they have in your group or church? Can you identify places where the life of the group, local community or church would be enriched by their practice? Are they the basis of a new society? What else needs to be included?

Reflection and Action

In your concern to become 'fishers of people' how can you be more effective in this task by the practice of the 'little virtues'? What foundations do you think you have laid for building a new community during the past few weeks?

This week marks the end of this particular series of themes. The next three themes are:

Christ the Teacher
Christ the Healer
Christ the Friend of Sinners.

Will you continue to meet as a group? What changes will you make to your plans? Have you unfinished work to do? How will you attend to it?

Before Lent

'In the past God spoke to our ancestors many times in many ways through the prophets, but in these last days he has spoken to us through his Son' (Hebrews 1:1). And that is how Theology started. People already knew about God in a vague way. Then came a man who claimed to be God; and yet he was not the sort of man you could dismiss as a lunatic – he made them believe in Him.

They met Him again after they had seen Him killed.

And then after they had formed a little society or community, they found God somehow inside them as well:

directing them, making them able to do things they could never do before.[5]

The three Sundays that precede **Lent** are known as the **Ninth, Eighth and Seventh Sundays before Easter**. The Christian faith is essentially a celebration of the triumph of good over evil. It is about *community* and *celebration* focused on the person of Jesus Christ, who loved God, and out of compassion and humanity brought healing and forgiveness for all.

The themes of the **Sundays before Easter** are:

> *Christ the Teacher*
> *Christ the Healer*
> *Christ the Friend of Sinners.*

Basic Preparation

As you begin *Seeds of the Word* for the Sundays before Easter, don't forget to reread pages 23–7. Agree **why, where** and **how** you are meeting; also decide on the allocation of **ministries**. **The Liturgical Colour** for this season is **green**.

Creating a focus

Jesus described himself as *the Way, the Truth, and the Life*. Take this theme as the subject of your group focus. You might make a small banner; or create some collage which reflects this theme, or use symbols such as: stones – *the Way*, the Bible – *the Truth*, and spring flowers – *the Life*.

Seasonal Collect:

> **Eternal God,**
> **whose Son Jesus Christ is for all humanity**
> **the way, the truth and the life:**
> **grant us to walk in his way,**
> **to rejoice in his truth,**
> **and to share his risen life;**

who is alive and reigns with you and the Holy Spirit,
one God, now and for ever. Amen.[6]

Ninth Sunday before Easter

Getting started

When you were at school who were the best teachers (and the
worst!)? Can you recall any one lesson you learnt at school?

Read Matthew 5:1–12.
(Other readings: Isaiah 30:18–21; 1 Corinthians 4:8–13.)

1   Seeing the crowds, Jesus went onto the mountain. And when
2   he was seated his disciples came to him. Then he began to
    speak. This is what he taught them:
3   How blessed are the poor in spirit: the kingdom of
        Heaven is theirs.
4   Blessed are the gentle: they shall have the earth as
        inheritance.
5   Blessed are those who mourn: they shall be comforted.
6   Blessed are those who hunger and thirst for uprightness;
        they shall have their fill.
7   Blessed are the merciful: they shall have mercy shown
        them.
8   Blessed are the pure in heart: they shall see God.
9   Blessed are the peacemakers: they shall be recognised
        as children of God.
10   Blessed are those who are persecuted in the cause of
        uprightness: the kingdom of Heaven is theirs.

11 Blessed are you when people abuse you and persecute you
    and speak all kinds of calumny against you falsely on my
12 account. Rejoice and be glad, for your reward will be great
    in heaven; this is how they persecuted the prophets before
    you.

Comment

Gandhi and Karl Marx both recognised the significance of chapters 5 and 6 of Matthew's Gospel. This series of the teachings of Jesus are often called 'the Sermon on the Mount'. What they reveal is that God's love is 'directed not simply toward humanity in general, but especially toward the victims of human unkindness [the poor or broken in spirit], the disadvantaged [the sick, landless, exploited], those who always come in last, who especially need comfort and affection [the hungry, the homeless, the discriminated against, and the unjustly treated].'[7]

Jesus says, 'Take God seriously. This world is not as God created it to be. Discipline yourselves to work for what God wants, namely a humanity in which justice, peace and harmony meet.' Jesus seeks to inspire courage and action, 'for unless power is awarded to the powerless, hope to the despairing, and light to those who dwell on the shadow side of life, no effective collaboration in the saving of the world can be expected.'[8]

This is a very down-to-earth passage. In Hebrew, the word for 'heaven' can also be translated 'God'. God is concerned that very ordinary things should indicate to people God's realm (or Kingdom) is very near – if people want it to be. For every time hungry people are fed, or sad people are consoled, or crying people laugh, or hate gives way to love, God's realm comes close. Some translations use the word 'happy' instead of 'blessed'. People *are* happy when they recognise the need for their lives to be reordered to work for a reordering of creation.

People who mourn because of evil and injustice, and begin to work for change, do *become* happy. When people act like this, they begin to discover that to be meek means to see all life as belonging to God. Violence, the opposite of meekness, requires greed and power to achieve its ends. Having 'the earth as inheritance' means recognising that 'the earth *is* the Lord's' (Psalm 24:1), and that those who exploit people and resources for their own ends violate the meek.

Talking Points

This is a call to action. The key lies in the invitation to become peacemakers (v. 9). In the 'Declaration on the Relationship of the Church to Judaism' (28 March 1980), the German bishops said, 'Christians and Jews together can and should advocate what in Hebrew is called *shalom. Shalom* means peace, joy, freedom, reconciliation, community, harmony, righteousness, truth, communication, humanity.'

In what ways are you as a group, or as individuals, practising *shalom*? Make a list.

Reflection and Action

If God's love is directed 'toward the victims of human unkindness, the disadvantaged, those who always come in last, who especially need comfort and affection', how will you as a group take steps to demonstrate this more effectively?

Worship

Use the Liturgy for Justice in the Resources for Worship (p. 241).

As you prepare for next week, focus on the people you know about who are sick, victims of disease or famine. Make a list and bring it with you. The **worship co-ordinator** should prepare a small amount of olive oil in a shallow container, and bring a Bible.

Eighth Sunday before Easter

Getting started

Share with the others in the group the list of suffering people you have made. Explain briefly why you are concerned. When all have shared sit, or kneel, placing your list in front of you. The **worship co-ordinator** will take the olive oil, and dipping a finger into the oil, mark the sign of the cross on the person next to him or her saying, 'May God heal and forgive.' The co-ordinator then passes the container on to the next person who repeats the process; do this until everyone has been anointed and prayed for. Conclude your worship with prayers and by reading James 5:13–16.

Read Mark 2:1–12.
(Other readings: Zephaniah 3:14-end; James 5:13–16a.)

1 When Jesus returned to Capernaum, some time later word
2 went round that he was in the house; and so many people
   collected that there was no room left, even in front of the
3 door. He was preaching the word to them when some people
4 came bringing him a paralytic carried by four men, but as
   they could not get the man to him through the crowd, they
   stripped the roof over the place where Jesus was; and when
   they had made an opening, they lowered the stretcher on
5 which the paralytic lay. Seeing their faith, Jesus said to the
6 paralytic, 'My child, your sins are forgiven.' Now some scribes
7 were sitting there, and they thought to themselves, 'How can
   this man talk like that? He is being blasphemous. Who but
8 God can forgive sins?' And at once, Jesus, inwardly aware
   that this is what they were thinking, said to them, 'Why do
9 you have these thoughts in your hearts? Which of these is
   easier: to say to the paralytic, "Your sins are forgiven" or to
10 say, "Get up, pick up your stretcher and walk"? But to prove
   to you that the Son of man has authority to forgive sins on
11 earth' – he said to the paralytic – 'I order you: get up, pick
12 up your stretcher, and go off home.' And the man got up,
   and at once picked up his stretcher and walked out in front
   of everyone, so that they were all astonished and praised God
   saying, 'We have never seen anything like this.'

Comment

Wheelchair-bound people are increasingly demanding access to places; and deaf people are insisting on having their unique signing language available in public meetings and places of entertainment. They are saying, 'We are differently abled from people who can walk, hear and speak; but we are not going to be excluded from places, or ideas, by others.' Modern societies still marginalise those they regard as 'sick' or 'disabled'.

In Jesus' time, disability and certain illnesses were regarded as being due either to a person's own sin or that of their parents. The religious law of the time denied the sick and disabled access to religious rites and status. The religious leaders regarded them as 'sinners', whether or not they had committed any immoral act, or broken the commandments. Unless they were 'healed', lepers, paralytics, people with blood disorders, skin complaints, blindness, and a whole host of other illnesses could not be fully accepted into 'the people of God'. Others, like tanners, shepherds, goldsmiths, dung collectors, manicurists, hairdressers, tax collectors – to name a few – were excluded too; they were 'sinners' because through the things they touched in the course of their work, they were regarded as polluted.

Healing the paralytic, Jesus gestures at a system that denied such people the right to live fully in the community. Jesus says, 'true impediments to discipleship have nothing to do with physical impairment, but with spiritual and ideological disorders: Having eyes can you not see? Having ears can you not hear?'[9]

By taking sides, Jesus raises the stakes. In a highly charged atmosphere, he exposes the struggle between himself as the Human One (traditionally called 'Son of man', 2:10), and the rulers of the Jews. Jesus is 'wresting away from the scribal and priestly class their "authority on earth." '[10] Surrounded by the poor and sick, Jesus is not just a healer, but one who through his actions is attacking the structures that continue to oppress the sick and excluded.

Talking Points

How does our society marginalise different groups of people? Who? Does the idea of sickness being the result of sin have any credibility? Many Christians value services of prayer for healing. You might like to look again at James 5:13–16 for verification of this practice. Is it enough to pray for healing? What situations are you aware of that oppress people who are disabled, or suffer from various kinds of illness? What issues need to be addressed? By whom?

Reflection and Action
Report on any action you have taken as a group in seeking to demonstrate God's love to victims of human unkindness, the disadvantaged, or those in need of comfort or affection. Has anything in today's reflection and discussion given you ideas of what you could do next?

Worship
In preparation for next week's worship, think of someone you know who is in some way disadvantaged or in need of comfort and affection. Choose to spend a little time with them. Listen to their concerns, hopes, dreams. Prepare a short prayer, or choose something to read which expresses an aspect of their life that has touched you.

Seventh Sunday before Easter

Getting started
Spend a few moments sharing your experience of time spent with someone who is a concern for you. Light a candle. Offer the prayers and readings based on the lives of those who have been your concern this week.

Read Mark 2:13–17.
(Other readings: Hosea 14:17; Philemon 1–16.)
13 **Jesus went out again to the shore of the lake; and all the**
14 **people came to him, and he taught them. As he was walking along he saw Levi the son of Alphaeus sitting at the tax office, and he said to him, 'Follow me.' And he got up and followed him.**
15   **When Jesus was at dinner in his house, a number of tax**

collectors and sinners were also sitting at table with Jesus and his disciples; for there were many of them among his
16   followers. When the scribes of the Pharisee party saw him eating with sinners and tax collectors, they said to his disciples, 'Why does he eat with tax collectors and sinners?'
17   When Jesus heard this he said to them, 'It is not the healthy who need the doctor, but the sick. I came to call not the upright, but sinners.'

Comment

The company Jesus kept was regarded by the rabbis and teachers of the faith as disreputable. None of them would have shared meals or travelled with the common people, and certainly not with tax collectors of whom 'there were many among Jesus' followers' (v. 15). These people were social outcasts, though economically well off.

They were widely and justifiably regarded as dishonest. As servants of the Roman occupying power, they were shunned by all true Jews.

Going to dinner with Levi (or Matthew, as he is better known), Jesus breaks a taboo. By taking his disciples along with him (v. 15), he is saying to them, and to others, 'Everyone is equal before God. There are now only sinners on the road of discipleship.' The disciples of Jesus are learning a significant lesson – as well as getting a free lunch – that, if they want to follow Jesus, they must accept that there is no one who is outcast, or excluded. On many occasions Jesus reminds the disciples that his vision of the new faith community is inclusive (Mark 9:30–50). Jesus' attitude was a total contrast to the prevailing religious climate in which the Pharisees taught that true believers are identified by their separation.

The disciples selected so far in Jesus' mission, like the fishermen (see p. 63) and tax collectors, are all people who are economically secure. They are the middle class, those with some means; Jesus sees their potential for influencing and changing things and calls them in to solidarity. They must join the struggle for those who are excluded on the grounds of class, poverty, gender and social acceptability.

Talking Points

Jesus is described as 'Friend of sinners'. 'Sinners' for Jesus had a particular connotation. It referred to people who were regarded as outside of the community of faith; unequal before God. Much modern Western Christianity emphasises 'sin' as that which is personal, 'breaking the commandments' and the like. Clearly, good moral behaviour strengthens communities, but has our concern for morality and spirituality made the Church exclusive rather than inclusive?

Reflection and Action

Who are the modern-day equivalents of the tax collectors, paralytics, prostitutes? Are there people we should seek hospitality from, or offer hospitality to, in order to demonstrate all are equal before God? How will you do this? In what way does this fit into the tasks you have already agreed upon?

How are your plans for using Lent shaping up? *Seeds of the Word* for Lent follows a six-week programme designed to encourage you to share your story, reflect on your experience, look at your situation, take steps for action, and celebrate your participation in bringing in God's new order.

Celebration

This session marks the end of the 'Before Lent' programme. Why not plan a pancake party, thinking whom you might include to share this occasion with you?

LENT

Lent in English means 'spring'. It is a season which provides for discovering new life in God. In early Christian tradition the period leading up to the *pascha*, or Christian celebration of Passover, was a time for training candidates for baptism. An extended period of preparation for baptism was seen as essential in order to test their sincerity. Besides study and prayer, this was a time of *fasting*. Fasting is a freely made choice to deny oneself food, recreation or some pleasure in order to prepare to serve God more effectively. St Paul used the picture of the

athlete in training (1 Corinthians 9:24, 25) as an example of
what fasting meant for him in his service of God.

Lent is a time for renewed commitment. 'To see the suffering
of Christ is to waken, to have our eyes opened to the suffering of all humanity. Put theologically, it is said that in Christ
crucified God has entered into every aspect of human life –
even suffering and death.'[1]

The title for the themes in **Lent** is:

> *The King and the Kingdom*[2]

The themes for **Lent** in *The Alternative Service Book* are:

> *Temptation*
> *Conflict*
> *Suffering*
> *Transfiguration*
> *The Victory of the Cross*
> *The Way of the Cross*

Basic Preparation

As you begin *Seeds of the Word* for **Lent**, don't forget to reread
pages 23–7. Agree **why, where** and **how** you are meeting; also
decide on the allocation of **ministries**.

The Liturgical Colours for this season are **violet** or **purple**.
For **Palm Sunday** the colour is **red**.

Creating a Focus

The wilderness, or desert, marked the place where Jesus
struggled to discern the type and nature of his ministry. Why
not create a focus that represents wilderness. The use of shells,
items of cloth, a cross, and a symbolic use of the colours for
Lent, provide the possibility of creative use of the imagination.

Seasonal Collect:

> **Almighty and everlasting God,**
> **you hate nothing you have made**

and forgive the sins of those who are penitent.
Create and make in us new and contrite hearts,
that, lamenting our sins,
and acknowledging our wretchedness,
we may receive from you, the God of all mercy,
perfect forgiveness and peace;
through Jesus Christ our Lord. Amen.[3]

First Sunday in Lent

Getting started

When you are looking for some warmth and comfort in your
life, where do you go and what do you do? Where is the place
in which you have been most comfortable? Where have you
been most uncomfortable? What are you hoping for from these
gatherings in Lent?

Read Matthew 4:1–11.
(Other readings: Genesis 2:7–9; 3:1–7; Hebrews 2:14–end.)

Then Jesus was led by the Spirit out into the desert to be put
to the test by the devil. He fasted for forty days and forty
nights, after which he was hungry, and the tester came and
said to him, 'If you are Son of God, tell these stones to turn
into loaves.' But he replied, 'Scripture says:

Human beings live not on bread alone
but on every word that comes from the mouth of God.'

The devil then took him to the holy city and set him on the
parapet of the Temple. 'If you are Son of God,' he said,
'throw yourself down; for scripture says:

He has given his angels orders about you,
and they will carry you in their arms
in case you trip over a stone.'

Jesus said to him, 'Scripture also says:

Do not put the Lord your God to the test.'

Next, taking him to a very high mountain, the devil showed him all the kingdoms of the world and their splendour. And he said to him, 'I will give you all these, if you fall at my feet and do me homage.' Then Jesus replied, 'Away with you, Satan! For scripture says:

The Lord your God is the one to whom you must do homage, him alone you must serve.'

Then the devil left him, and suddenly angels appeared and looked after him.

Comment

The wilderness in Jewish tradition is a place of chaos, disorder and injustice. Jesus' baptism was a commitment to seek justice (Matthew 3:15; 6:33). The challenge of the wilderness for Jesus was how to *do* justice. Would Jesus be 'Beloved Son' (3:17), or seek power (v. 3), prestige (v. 5) and possessions (vv. 8–9) for himself, possibly at the expense of others?

Real temptations!

In history, Israel had come out of the wilderness, taken possession of the promised land, and then had forgotten the God who had 'brought them out of the land of Egypt, out of the land of bondage' (Deuteronomy 6:10, 16; 8:12–14). 'The Lord God was put to the test.' God wondered if it had all been worthwhile!

The values, ideals and decisions of Israel were dominated by the taking of land to acquire power and wealth. Very quickly the need for economic security became more important than trust in God. Yet God did not lose his vision: God wanted a community of people where possessions, power and prestige are shared. His dream was of an environment in which justice for all becomes possible, and realisable.

Jesus chose to reject the temptation of power, prestige and possessions, and opt for obedience to God's vision of community or 'household' (Hebrews 3:1–7). Such a vision would make possible a way of living in which the gifts of land, possessions and prestige are shared. The temptations that faced Jesus faced the church to whom Matthew wrote his Gospel fifty years later. The same temptations face the Church today.

Talking Points

Where are the places of chaos, disorder and injustice today? Where do we place our security? Is it in physical comfort and protection? In power over others? In intimacy with others? Who is God for us?

Reflection and Action

In what ways do you trust God day by day? Are you aware of any people who are dispossessed? Who needs the sharing of bread and possessions? What steps can you as a group take to create a more just way of living? Keep things local and simple. Decide who will do what and report progress next time.

Worship

Read the Gospel Matthew 4:1–11 again.

Say the Lord's Prayer. Keep a few minutes' silence for people to offer their own prayers.

For next week's worship invite some people to prepare prayers and readings on the theme of *Exploitation*.

Second Sunday in Lent

Getting started

During the past week who has evoked the most sympathy from you? Why? What has made you most angry? Why?

Read Luke 19:41-end.

(Other readings: Genesis 6:11-end; 1 John 4:1–6.)

41   As Jesus drew near and came in sight of the city, he shed

42   tears over it and said, 'If you too had only recognised on this

day the way to peace! But in fact it is hidden from your
43 eyes! Yes, a time is coming when your enemies will raise
fortifications all round you, when they will encircle you and
44 hem you in on every side: they will dash you and the children
inside your walls to the ground; they will leave not one stone
standing on another within you, because you did not recognise
the moment of your visitation.'
45   Then he went to the Temple and began driving out those
46 who were busy trading, saying to them, 'According to scripture, my house shall be a house of prayer but you have turned
it into a bandits' den.'
47   He taught in the Temple every day. The chief priests and
the scribes, in company with the leading citizens, tried to do
48 away with him, but they could not find a way to carry this
out because the whole people hung on his words.

Comment

Deep sympathy (v. 41) and anger (vv. 45–6). Two contrasting
emotions. Destruction is coming on Jerusalem by human enemies (vv. 43–4). The city will be besieged and its people punished
because of the powerful, a veritable 'bandits' den' (v. 46), 'chief
priests, scribes and leading citizens' (v. 47).

The action of driving out those who were busy trading (v.
45), 'overturning the tables' (Matthew 21:12–17), is a direct
challenge to the system and the power of the oppressors
(Malachi 3:5,8,10). The Temple itself robs the poor. The
oppressors 'tried to do away with him' (v. 47) but 'the whole
people hung on his words.' (Some translations use 'common
people'.)

The prophet Isaiah saw the Temple as a place of joy for the
common people, the social outcast and the foreigner (Isaiah
56:1–8). The prophet Jeremiah believed that Israel's special
relationship with God could only exist if justice towards the
foreigner, the fatherless, widows and the innocent was practised
(Jeremiah 7:5–7). If the nation exploited people and idolatry
was practised (Jeremiah 7:9–15), then the Temple would be

destroyed like the first shrine to Yahweh was at Shiloh. Such a destruction would be seen as an ending of the special relationship.

By his action against the traders, Jesus exposed the conflict between the rule, or domination-free order of God, and those who oppress the poor. Luke, by writing this account, exposes the Church to the challenge of living justly towards the poor and oppressed. And 'because there is no time of the church separated from the time of Jesus',[4] it challenges us today.

Talking Points

What situations in today's world make you want to weep? What makes you angry? Many middle-class Christians are generous with their time, money and service on behalf of the poor. When it comes to changing the terms of the relationship between rich and poor, few are willing to work for a redistribution of wealth that will make for a just social order. Why do you think this is? What can be done to change things?

Reflection and Action

How did the action you took last week work out? Has anything emerged from your discussion today that indicates what more can be done? What will you do next? Are you asking appropriate questions? (See page 26 for a reminder.) Decide who will do what and report progress.

Worship

Offer the worship you have planned on the theme of *Exploitation*.

Decide who will lead worship next time, and make your theme *The Cross*. Many people have crucifixes or crosses which they wear as jewellery – bring examples of these to incorporate into your worship. Say who gave you the cross, and why it means so much to you.

Third Sunday in Lent

Getting started

Have you ever been misunderstood in something you have
said, or done? What happened? How did you feel? Were you
able to resolve the misunderstanding?

Read Luke 9:18–27.
(Other readings: Genesis 22:1–13; Colossians 1:24-end.)

18 Now it happened that Jesus was praying alone, and his dis-
     ciples came to him and he put this question to them, 'Who
19 do the crowds say I am?' And they answered, 'Some say John
     the Baptist; others Elijah; others again one of the ancient
20 prophets come back to life.' 'But you,' he said to them, 'who
     do you say that I am?' It was Peter who spoke up. 'The Christ
21 of God,' he said. But he gave them strict orders and charged
     them not to say this to anyone.

22   He said, 'The Son of man is destined to suffer grievously,
     to be rejected by the elders and chief priests and scribes
     and to be put to death, and to be raised up on the third day.'

23   Then speaking to all, he said, 'If anyone wants to be a
     follower of mine, let him renounce himself and take up his
24 cross every day and follow me. Anyone who wants to save
     his life will lose it; but anyone who loses his life for my sake
25 will save it. What benefit is it to anyone to win the whole
26 world and forfeit or lose his very self? For if anyone is
     ashamed of me and of my words, of him the Son of man will
     be ashamed when he comes in his own glory and in the glory
     of the Father and the holy angels.

27   'I tell you truly, there are some standing here who will not
     taste death before they see the kingdom of God.'

Comment

'Who do you say that I am?' (v. 20) It mattered to Jesus that
people following him knew who he was and what he was about.
Peter gave a 'correct' answer (v. 20) which was apparently

acceptable (v. 21). In Luke's Gospel, Jesus expands the disciples' understanding: 'The Son of man is destined to suffer grievously . . . to be put to death, and to be raised up on the third day' (v. 22). In Mark (8:31–3) and Matthew (16:21–3) Jesus rejects their interpretation of what it means to be 'Christ of God': 'You are thinking not as God thinks, but as human beings do' (Mark 8:33).

As an advocate of true justice Jesus was frequently and inevitably in conflict with the authorities (Mark 8:31). Jesus taught publicly that to follow him meant denying self and taking up the cross. Crucifixion was a political and military punishment reserved for people with no rights: dissidents, slaves, rebels and the lower classes. The cross revealed the true nature of the conflict and the suffering which Jesus invited people to face with him. It was to be treated as the lowest of the low.

Discipleship is determined by the willingness to face the paradox of the gospel, *'to save one's life'* or *'to lose it'*. With the death penalty the state was able to create fear, thereby keeping itself as the dominant power. On the cross, Jesus was mocked for 'saving others' (Mark 15:31), and losing his own life.

When the chips were down, others had their price – Peter (Mark 14:31), Judas (Mark 14:11) and the rich man (Mark 10:21f.), to name but three. Those who want to be followers of Jesus in many parts of the world today continue to face the same risks, interrogation by the state authorities, and identification with 'subversives'. Small wonder Jesus asked, *'Who do you think you are following?'*

Talking Points

'I don't think we Christians have understood what carrying the cross means: the path of baptism. We are not carrying the cross when we are poor or sick, or suffering small everyday things. They are all part of life. The cross comes when we try to change things. That is how it came for Jesus.' Do you agree with these words from Fr Miguel D'Escoto of Nicaragua? Can you think of examples in your own or other people's lives that would bear this out?

Reflection and Action
How has today's study helped you understand what the cross is really about? Has it helped you to understand difficulties you may have encountered? How?

Report on progress with your group community action so far. Do you need more information, help, re-evaluation? Where will you get it? What is your next task?

Worship
Offer your act of worship on the theme of *The cross*.

Next week each group member should bring a candle and something to hold it in. Ask each person to prepare a prayer on the theme of *My discipleship*. During the worship, place the candles in the shape of a cross on the floor; as each person places their candle, let them offer their prayer, silently or aloud. Arrange for someone to bring a tape or disc of music for the group to listen at the Passiontide sessions.

Fourth Week in Lent

Getting started
Where is the place in your life that you have felt closest to God? Share as much of your experience as you can.

Read Luke 9:28–36.
(Other readings: Exodus 34:29-end; 2 Corinthians 3:4-end.)

28   Now about eight days after this had been said, he took with
     him Peter, John and James and went up the mountain to
29   pray. And it happened that, as he was praying, the aspect of
     his face was changed and his clothing became sparkling white.
30   And suddenly there were two men talking to him; they were
31   Moses and Elijah appearing in glory, and they were speaking

32 of his passing which he was to accomplish in Jerusalem. Peter
    and his companions were heavy with sleep, but they woke
33 up and saw his glory and the two men standing with him. As
    these were leaving him, Peter said to Jesus, 'Master, it is
    wonderful for us to be here; so let us make three shelters,
    one for you, one for Moses and one for Elijah.' He did not
34 know what he was saying. As he was saying this, a cloud
    came and covered them with shadow; and when they went
35 into the cloud the disciples were afraid. And a voice came
    from the cloud saying, 'This is my Son, the Chosen One.
36 Listen to him.' And after the voice had spoken, Jesus was
    found alone. The disciples kept silence and, at that time, told
    no one what they had seen.

Comment

Mountains are places for meeting God. When a life-threatening
path had to be trodden Jesus, like everyone, needed encouragement. On the mountain top Peter, James and John are witnesses
to a conference between Moses, Elijah and Jesus. Together
they hear 'a voice from the clouds' (v. 35) and are reduced to
silence.

Elijah and Moses were both people of the mountain. Elijah
was in trouble with the authorities and went to the mountains
to seek refuge. He was given strength and returned by God to
the struggle (1 Kings 19:11ff.). The presence of Elijah evoked
memories of John the Baptist (Matthew 11:14). His political
and pastoral ministry also resulted in trial and execution. Moses
too climbed mountains and on Mount Sinai was given the
commandments of God, which were to create a just nation.
When the people subsequently rejected God's commandments,
Moses returned to the mountain (Exodus 33:18ff.) devastated
by the rejection.

Mountains reveal. The dazzling whiteness of the robes is
symbolic; its significance would not have been entirely lost on
the disciples, but would have reminded them of the martyrs
(Revelation 3:5, 18; 4:4; 6:11; 7:9, 13), of the resurrection (Mark

16:5), of Moses and of Elijah. They wanted a memorial to the event (9:33). But poor old things, again they have misunderstood the significance of the moment. It was all in the voice – the voice which spoke on Sinai, and in the stillness to Elijah, now spoke the words given at the baptism once again, 'This is my Son, the Chosen One' – adding, 'Listen to him' (cf. Mark 1:11).

Listening to the voice requires the hearer to understand that there is no discipleship without taking up the cross.

Talking Points
Where do you look for encouragement when you have to make tough decisions? Who in your life always makes you face the difficulties rather than avoid them? Jesus didn't get gathered up to heaven at the transfiguration, but like Elijah was sent back to complete the task. 'The gospel is not a message of salvation of individuals from the world, but a message of a world transfigured right down to its basic structures.'5 Do we know whom we are following and what he is about?

Reflection and Action
Using the group **memory** and other reflections review the past four weeks. How has your meeting together helped build expectant faith that God is at work in you and others? Has your understanding of the cross changed? How? How has the cross affected your lives as a group? What are the next steps for you as a group as an agency of change? What have you to celebrate?

Worship
Offer your worship on '*My discipleship*', as suggested last time.

Plan a short act of worship for next time on the theme *Mountains*. Ask people to share some encounter with God that could be called 'a mountain-top experience'. Read Psalm 121 and offer prayers of thanksgiving.

PASSIONTIDE

Fifth Sunday in Lent

Getting started

Begin by sharing mountain-top experiences! Follow this with an act of worship as suggested last week.

Read John 12:20–32.
(Other readings: Exodus 6:2–13; Colossians 2:8–15.)

20 Among those who went up to worship at the festival were
21 some Greeks. These approached Philip, who came from

Bethsaida in Galilee, and put this request to him, 'Sir, we
22 should like to see Jesus.' Philip went to tell Andrew, and
Andrew and Philip together went to tell Jesus.

23   Jesus replied to them:

> Now the hour has come
> for the Son of man to be glorified.

24   In all truth I tell you,
> unless a grain of wheat falls into the earth and dies,
> it remains only a single grain;
> but if it dies
> it yields a rich harvest.

25   Anyone who loves his life loses it;
> anyone who hates his life in this world
> will keep it for eternal life.

26   Whoever serves me, must follow me,
> and my servant will be with me wherever I am.
> If anyone serves me, my Father will honour him.

27   Now my soul is troubled.
> What shall I say:
> Father, save me from this hour?
> But it is for this very reason that I have come to this
>   hour.

28   Father, glorify your name!

A voice came from heaven, 'I have glorified it, and I will
again glorify it.'

29   The crowd standing by, who heard this, said it was a clap
30 of thunder; others said, 'It was an angel speaking to him.'
Jesus answered, 'It was not for my sake that this voice came,
but for yours.

31   'Now sentence is being passed on this world;
> now the prince of this world is to be driven out.

32   And when I am lifted up from the earth,
> I shall draw all people to myself.'

Comment

The Gospel of John confronts readers with the question, 'Where does your allegiance lie – with Jesus, or with the world?' The people who first read the Gospel seem to have believed that followers of Jesus should form communities that acted as a sort of counter-culture to the prevailing trends (v. 26). The members of these communities would be recognised by their 'love for one another' (John 13:34–5).

John's communities experienced violence, persecution and hatred (John 15:18–25). Their belief in Jesus gave clear understanding of the struggle such communities faced – it was light against darkness (John 12:46) – God's will against human will; 'Jesus' over against 'the world'. 'The "world" is not the world of creation – "nature" as such, of earth and sky, sexuality and labour, health and sickness . . . In short, it is human society as such, as it is organised and maintained for the good of some, but to the harm of others and to the detriment of the love of God.'[1]

Jesus knew the cost of challenging the status quo, and he put it in stark terms: 'Anyone who loves his life loses it; anyone who hates his life in this world will keep it' (v. 25). Criticising injustice and enabling 'sentence to be passed on this world' (v. 31) is the radical demand, and it has its price. Just as a rich harvest cannot come unless 'a grain of wheat falls into the earth and dies' (v. 24), neither can real change take place without cost.

John affirms clearly that Jesus is 'the Saviour of the world' – no imperial powers can save it. Even though Roman emperors called themselves 'Lord and God', John insists that this title is only appropriate for the Christ who 'shall draw all people' to himself (v. 31).

Talking Points

Are the choices between God and the world as stark today? How is contemporary Christianity providing a critique of secular society and its oppressive and ungodly structures? What signs are there of communities of resistance within the Christian Church?

Reflection and Action
John believed that communities of faith demonstrating self-giving love were the most effective way of resisting and criticising the violence and injustice of 'the world'. What marks of such a community does your group have? What more are you looking for? Plan your future as a group to be more faithful to the vision of Jesus as expressed in John.

Worship
Holy Week begins with Palm Sunday. Bring a Palm Cross to your next meeting. Share with the group what the cross has come to symbolise for you. The group should lay their crosses on the floor, or a table, to form the shape of a cross. Say the following prayer together:

> Merciful God,
> We meet each other today
> at this cross as the inhabitants of one world.
> We wait with each other
> as those who inflict wounds on each other:
> Be merciful to us.
> Amen.[2]

Palm Sunday

Getting started
Have you ever participated in a demonstration? What were you demonstrating about? How did you feel? What did you hope to achieve? Was it successful?

Read Matthew 21:1–14.
(Other readings: Zechariah 9:9–12; 1 Corinthians 1:18–25.)
1   When they were near Jerusalem and had come to Bethphage

2   on the Mount of Olives, then Jesus sent two disciples, saying
     to them, 'Go to the village facing you, and you will at once
     find a tethered donkey and a colt with her. Untie them and
3   bring them to me. If anyone says anything to you, you are to
     say, "The Master needs them and will send them back at
4   once." ' This was to fulfil what was spoken by the prophet:

5   Say to the daughter of Zion:
         Look, your king is approaching,
         humble and riding on a donkey
         and on a colt, the foal of a beast of burden.

6, 7 So the disciples went and did as Jesus had told them. • They
     brought the donkey and the colt, then they laid their cloaks
8   on their backs and he took his seat on them. Great crowds
     of people spread their cloaks on the road, while others were
9   cutting branches from the trees and spreading them in his
     path. The crowds who went in front of him and those who
     followed were all shouting:

         Hosanna to the son of David!
         Blessed is he who is coming in the name of the Lord!
         Hosanna in the highest heavens!

10   And when he entered Jerusalem, the whole city was in tur-
11   moil as people asked, 'Who is this?' and the crowds answered,
     'This is the prophet Jesus from Nazareth in Galilee.'
12   Jesus then went into the Temple and drove out all those
     who were selling and buying there; he upset the tables of the
13   money-changers and the seats of the dove-sellers. He said to
     them, 'According to scripture, my house will be called a house
14   of prayer; but you are turning it into a bandits' den.' There
     were also blind and lame people who came to him in the
     Temple, and he cured them.

Comment

Protest or street theatre? Sometimes the two go together. The
demonstration was well planned (vv. 1–6). Jesus 'acted out' the

prophet's words (vv. 4–5). As with many demonstrations, there is an element of farce. Conquering kings rode in triumph into cities, with cart-loads of booty they had collected, and a procession of captives. Jesus, on the other hand, is the king with no possessions, 'nowhere to lay his head' (Luke 9:57–8; Matthew 8:19–20). By riding a borrowed donkey, Jesus appears to be deliberately parodying military solutions. His actions in the Temple (vv. 11–13) demonstrate that he is not going to fight to defend the Temple state. 'His entry into Jerusalem attracted attention, "humble [or meek], and riding on a donkey" acted as a reminder to the authorities that "Happy are the meek, for they shall inherit the earth" ' (Matthew 5:4). Meekness, far from being weakness, recognises that all life is grounded in God. The crowd, made up of the peasantry, are the first to recognise this 'prophet . . . from Galilee' (v. 11), while visitors ask the questions (v. 10) and the authorities become ill at ease.

The Temple was a symbol of economic, political and spiritual power. The Temple was being redeveloped by the 'crafty, paranoid and repressive Herod, the Roman client king whose heavy taxes had won him few friends among the common folk. His development project of the Temple was a shrewd public relations manoeuvre to cover up Jewish public opinion.'[3] The Temple, built on the backs of the poor, acted as a bank. It also contained the debt records of small farmers who could not pay their tithe to the landowners, and who frequently borrowed money at extortionate rates to pay their dues. (In the civil war of AD 66, when the Zealots entered Jerusalem, they broke into the strong room and burnt these debt records.)

Jesus' action (vv. 12–13) symbolically closed down the Temple. His vision is of a Jerusalem – meaning *vision of peace* – which must become a place where the alien, fatherless, widows and innocent can find justice (Jeremiah 7:5–7). For a brief, glorious moment the vision comes true and the blind and lame are cured (v. 14).

Talking Points
The poor, the sick, women, children, and certain classes of workers, like shepherds, tanners, doctors and many others, were regarded as second-class citizens in first-century Palestine. They were obliged 'to make reparation through sacrifices – for their inferior status.'[4] Jesus had seen how the Temple system broke the widow (Mark 12:41ff.). Who are the second-class citizens in your country? In your church? How are they exploited, taken advantage of, or excluded?

Reflection and Action
As Jesus confronted the structures of power, the hostility towards him grew. During the past few weeks, as you have sought to bring about some change, what hostility have you faced? How will you work to end second-class citizenship among those you have identified? How far are you prepared to go? Jesus had a moment of triumph (v. 14) in giving back the Temple to the oppressed. Have there been any such moments in your recent experience together?

Worship
Offer the worship suggested last meeting.
  This marks the end of *Seeds* for Lent. You need to decide how you will continue as a group. **Good Friday** marks the culmination of Jesus' struggle with the powers. Why not meet as a group on Good Friday evening and reflect on your struggle? *Seeds of the Word* for Good Friday gives a focus for such a gathering. Look at it now and plan how you will use the time together.

Good Friday

Getting started
Bring a symbol of hope – something that speaks to you about hope and future. Begin with a simple meal, such as Good Friday (fish and vegetable) soup and Hot Cross buns. Create a

focus for the evening. During the meal, discuss how you have
spent today. Do you have any stories about the commemor-
ation of Good Friday when you were younger? Share your
symbol and its meaning.

Read Mark 15:22–41.
In today's study take particular care to read the additional
references, so that the full impact of the crucifixion and its
implications for us are realised.

22   **They brought Jesus to the place called Golgotha, which
        means the place of the skull.**

23   **They offered him wine mixed with myrrh, but he refused
24   it. Then they crucified him and shared out his clothing,
25   casting lots to decide what each should get. It was the third
26   hour when they crucified him. The inscription giving the
27   charge against him read, 'The King of the Jews'. And they
        crucified two bandits with him, one on his right and one on
        his left.**

29   **The passers-by jeered at him; they shook their heads and
        said, 'Aha! So you would destroy the Temple and rebuild
30   it in three days! Then save yourself; come down from the
31   cross!' The chief priests and the scribes mocked him among
        themselves in the same way with the words, 'He saved
32   others, he cannot save himself. Let the Christ, the king of
        Israel, come down from the cross now, for us to see it and
        believe.' Even those who were crucified with him taunted
        him.**

33   **When the sixth hour came there was darkness over the
34   whole land until the ninth hour. And at the ninth hour
        Jesus cried out in a loud voice, '*Eloi, eloi, lama sabach-
        thani?*', which means, 'My God, my God, why have you
35   forsaken me?' When some of those who stood by heard
36   this, they said, 'Listen, he is calling on Elijah.' Someone
        ran and soaked a sponge in vinegar and, putting it on a
        reed, gave it to him to drink, saying, 'Wait! And see if
37, 38 Elijah will come to take him down.' But Jesus gave a loud**

39   cry and breathed his last. • And the veil of the Sanctuary was torn in two from top to bottom. The centurion, who was standing in front of him, had seen how he had died, and he said, 'In truth this man was Son of God.'

40   There were some women watching from a distance. Among them Mary of Magdala, Mary who was the mother

41   of James the younger and Joset, and Salome. These used to follow him and look after him when he was in Galilee. And many other women were there who had come up to Jerusalem with him.

Comment

'Then they crucified him'. No other words would have been necessary to convey the horror of this form of execution to Mark's readers. The tortured, defeated man is paraded through the streets (v. 21) surrounded by the panoply of imperial power. Those crucified usually died of asphyxiation, if they had not been torn to bits by wild animals. The inscription 'King of the Jews' becomes cynical mockery, a sign of Caesar's inscription and power (Mark 12:13–17). The places of honour, 'one on his right, one on his left' (10:37), are taken by bandits. Jesus is verbally abused, first by the Jews, 'So you would destroy the Temple and rebuild it in three days! Save yourself' (v. 30); then by the priests (v. 31); and finally 'even those who were crucified with him taunted him' (v. 32). 'It is as if the whole of Palestinian political culture has issued a rejection of the way of Jesus.'[5]

Jesus cries out (v. 34). The crowd waits for a rescue bid (v. 36). Heaven is silent this time (cf. Mark 1:9–11; 9:2–8). The final agonized cry, then the silence of death (v. 37). What has happened to the promise that Jesus made? 'There are some standing here who will not taste death before they see the kingdom of God come with power' (9:1; 14:62). In Mark's account, clues exist to the answer. First, 'when the sixth hour came there was darkness' (v. 33). The sun, a cosmic symbol, disappears. Second, 'the veil of the Sanctuary was torn in two from top to bottom' (v. 38). The veil symbolised the old religious and political order. These two signs represent the old order being overthrown (13:24–37).

The people who witness 'the kingdom come with power' are the women representatives of the disciples (v. 40), a group from the Sanhedrin (v. 31) and the Romans (v. 39). But this is only for those with the eye of faith, for in reality defeat by the Romans and the Sanhedrin is plain for all to see. The Roman soldier's recognition of who Jesus was (v. 39), and the removal of the body by a member of the Sanhedrin, Joseph, do not take away any of their complicity in the structures that brought about Jesus' execution. Jesus has always been known by 'name' to demons and political opponents alike (3:11; 5:7; 6:3; 14:61). The centurion 'names' him after death; and Joseph is more concerned for ritual purity, that a dead body does not defile the Sabbath. 'The one who claimed to be "Lord over the Sabbath" (2:28) is subjected to the ultimate insult – improper entombment [un-anointed and improperly wrapped] – for the sake of Sabbath order.'[6] However much Christian piety would like to make the centurion and Joseph icons of repentance, the evidence at this point does not stack up.

Finally, the male disciples too are missing. The women from Galilee who followed and served Jesus, and were in at the beginning of the story (1:31), are in at the end. 'The women have done two things that the males in the community have found impossible: they have been servants, and they continued to follow Jesus even after he was arrested and executed. The world order is being overturned from the highest political power to the deepest cultural patterns, and it begins with the new community.'[7]

Talking Points and Reflection
No evil can hold sway for ever. Look at events in recent years, where evil systems or structures have been overcome – add your own ideas or persons to this list: the emancipation of slaves; Martin Luther King; the end of apartheid in South Africa; the fall of the Berlin Wall; Tiananmen Square.

Despite the dreadful nature of the crucifixion, Mark's Gospel points to a new age coming when the powers that hurt and destroy shall be overcome. How can you take heart from this hope? What has today's Comment helped you to see about Good Friday that you had not seen before?

Worship
Close your gathering by saying together:

Lord:
help us to see in the groaning of creation
not death throes but birth pangs;
help us to see in suffering a promise for the future,
because it is a cry against the inhumanity of the present.
Help us to glimpse in protest the dawn of justice,
in the Cross the pathway to resurrection,
and in suffering the seeds of joy.[8]

Happy Easter!

EASTER

Easter is *the* Christian festival. It celebrates the triumph of life over death, good over evil, forgiveness over retribution. It begins with a displaced stone at the opening of a tomb. The first witnesses to the *persona* of the risen Christ are women whose testimony in a court of law at the time had no validity. Yet the event that marks out the central hope of Christian people through the centuries – **Christ is risen** – is testified to throughout the Gospel narratives by a woman. 'The world order is being overturned, from the highest political power to the deepest cultural patterns, and it begins with the new community. It will be these women, the "last" become "first", who will be entrusted with the resurrection message.'[1]

Easter is a time of celebration, of encouragement and hope. It is the season that shouts: *Christ has died, Christ is risen, Christ will come again.* There is a better way – who will follow?

The themes for the **Sundays after Easter** in *The Alternative Service Book* are as much about places as people:

> *The Garden*
> *The Upper Room*
> *The Emmaus Road*
> *The Lakeside*

Basic Preparation

As you begin *Seeds of the Word* for the **Easter** season, don't forget to reread pages 23–7. Agree **why**, **where** and **how** you are meeting; also decide on the allocation of **ministries.**

The Liturgical Colours for this season are **white** or **gold**.

Creating a Focus

Making an Easter garden is something which happens in many churches. You may feel something similar would make a good focus for your group. The locations of the Garden, Upper Room, Emmaus Road, or the Galilee Lakeside may prompt more imaginative ideas. Individuals may wish to bring symbols of their own faith journey that are appropriate to the season.

Seasonal Collect:

> **Lord of all life and power,**
> **who through the mighty resurrection of your Son**
> **overcame the old order of sin and death**
> **to make all things new in him:**
> **grant that we, being dead to sin**
> **and alive to you in Jesus Christ,**
> **may reign with him in glory;**
> **to whom with you and the Holy Spirit**

be praise and honour, glory and might,
now and in all eternity. Amen.[2]

Easter Day

Getting started
Whose death or funeral has had the greatest impact on your
life? Why?

Read John 20:1–18.
(Other readings: Isaiah 12:1; 1 Corinthians 15:12–20.)

1   It was very early on the first day of the week and still dark,
     when Mary of Magdala came to the tomb. She saw that the
2   stone had been moved away from the tomb and came running
     to Simon Peter and the other disciple, the one whom Jesus
     loved. 'They have taken the Lord out of the tomb,' she said,
     'and we don't know where they have put him.'
3   So Peter set out with the other disciple to go to the tomb.
4   They ran together, but the other disciple, running faster than
5   Peter, reached the tomb first; he bent down and saw the linen
6   cloths lying on the ground, but did not go in. Simon Peter,
     following him, also came up and went into the tomb, saw the
7   linen cloths lying on the ground and also the cloth that had
     been over his head; this was not with the linen cloths but
8   rolled up in a place by itself. Then the other disciple who
     had reached the tomb first also went in; he saw and he
9   believed. Till this moment they had still not understood the
10   scripture, that he must rise from the dead. The disciples then
     went back home.
11   But Mary was standing outside near the tomb, weeping.
12   Then, as she wept, she stooped to look inside, and saw two
     angels in white sitting where the body of Jesus had been, one
13   at the head, the other at the feet. They said, 'Woman, why
     are you weeping?' 'They have taken my Lord away,' she
14   replied, 'and I don't know where they have put him.' As
     she said this she turned round and saw Jesus standing there,

15 though she did not realise that it was Jesus. Jesus said to her,
    'Woman, why are you weeping? Who are you looking for?'
    Supposing him to be the gardener, she said, 'Sir, if you have
    taken him away, tell me where you have put him, and I will
16 go and remove him.' Jesus said, 'Mary!' She turned round
    and then said to him in Hebrew, 'Rabbuni' – which means
17 Master. Jesus said to her, 'Do not cling to me, because I have
    not yet ascended to the Father. But go to the brothers, and
    tell them: I am ascending to my Father and your Father, to
18 my God and to your God.' So Mary of Magdala told the
    disciples, 'I have seen the Lord,' and that he had said these
    things to her.

Comment

A woman's witness was not valid in a Jewish court of law. Mary
Magdalene gives evidence to Peter and the 'other disciple',
probably John, that 'they have taken the Lord out of the tomb'.
A race ensues, John arrives first 'but did not go in.' Peter
plunders in, sums up the evidence of human activity in rolled-
up grave clothes, and leaves. John enters and allegedly 'he saw
and he believed' (v. 9). But what did he believe? The narrator
goes on to say, 'they had still not understood the scripture, that
he must rise from the dead' (v. 10). The evidence points to
John 'believing' Mary Magdalene's evidence that the tomb was
empty. 'Before we infer too much, the narrator stops us and
makes clear that resurrection faith continues to elude even the
most faithful of followers.'[3]

The apathetic and confused male disciples leave Mary alone,
comfortless and weeping at the empty tomb. Returning into
the tomb, she experiences a vision of two angels 'sitting
where the body of Jesus had been, one at the head, and the
other at the feet' (v. 12). The discarded headcloth (*soudarion*),
which was used to wipe sweat away, and wrap the head of the
corpse, lies in the grave. It is not needed any more. Because
of the hurried burial, only the feet of Jesus were anointed with
embalming spices (John 12:3). 'Both the sacred (anointing oil)

and the profane (*soudarion*) objects of death are replaced by radiant signs of eternal life.'[4]

Later in the garden Mary turns twice (vv. 14 and 16) to speak to the same person. There is recognition, Jesus says to her, 'Mary!' She replies, 'Teacher.' 'Her turning is not so much a spin on her heels but a *metanoia*, a conversion of heart.'[5]

Talking Points

Is there an experience in your life where something good has come out of something apparently hopeless? Mary was asked, 'Why are you weeping?' Who are the people you know who are weeping? Why? Mary was also asked, 'Who are you looking for?' Answer this question as a group. What do you need God to be for you as an individual, or group? In what ways can you echo Mary's declaration, 'I have seen the Lord'. Share your experiences.

Reflection and Action

If we are to be part of the process of change, we ourselves need to accept change. During the next few days try and create space for yourself. Ask, 'Who am I looking for? Why am I weeping? How have I seen the Lord?' Think about how you can share some of your insights with the group next time you meet.

Worship

Begin by using the following prayer:

> God, you are doing a new thing in our world,
> leading us along new paths of mutual discovery,
> joint learning,
> exchange and encounter,
> calling us to cross barriers of prejudice,
> fear,
> anxiety.
> Lead us on into your new world
> as the new people of God,

with Jesus Christ our partner and pioneer.
Amen.[6]

Reread the Gospel John 20:1–18. Say the Lord's Prayer.
Close by saying:

> 'Peace be with you.
> As the Father sent me,
> so I am sending you.'

For next week's **Worship**:

Read the Gospel John 20:19–29. Ask someone to write a few
short prayers with the response 'Peace be with you'.

Use as a blessing to be said together:

> 'As the Father sent me
> so I am sending you.
> Receive the Holy Spirit.'

Close with sharing the peace:

LEADER: You believe because you can see me.
PEOPLE: Blessed are those who have not seen, yet believe.
LEADER: We have seen the Lord.
PEOPLE: Peace be with you.

The First Sunday after Easter

Getting started
Begin by sharing some of the insights you have had in response
to the questions, 'Who am I looking for? For whom am I
weeping? How have I seen the Lord?'

Read John 20:19–29.
(Other readings: Exodus 15:1–11; 1 Peter 1:3–9.)

**19 In the evening of that same day, the first day of the week,
    the doors were closed in the room where the disciples were,
    for fear of the Jews. Jesus came and stood among them. He**

20   said to them, 'Peace be with you,' and after saying this, he
      showed them his hands and his side. The disciples were filled
21   with joy at seeing the Lord and he said to them again, 'Peace
      be with you.

            'As the Father sent me
            so am I sending you.'

22   After saying this he breathed on them and said:

            Receive the Holy Spirit.
23   If you forgive anyone's sins,
            they are forgiven;
            if you retain anyone's sins
            they are retained.

24   Thomas, called the Twin, who was one of the Twelve, was
25   not with them when Jesus came. So the other disciples said
      to him, 'We have seen the Lord,' but he answered, 'Unless I
      can see the holes that the nails made in his hands and can
      put my finger into the holes they made, and unless I can put
26   my hand into his side, I refuse to believe.' Eight days later
      the disciples were in the house again and Thomas was with
      them. The doors were closed, but Jesus came in and stood
27   among them. 'Peace be with you,' he said. Then he spoke to
      Thomas, 'Put your finger here; look, here are my hands. Give
      me your hand; put it into my side. Do not be unbelieving any
28   more, but believe.' Thomas replied, 'My Lord and my God!'
29   Jesus said to him:

            You believe because you can see me.
            Blessed are those who have not seen and yet believe.

Comment

The community is in shock, but it is still together. The dispersal
of Peter and John 'back home' (v. 10) earlier in the day has
given way to a fearful gathering in the Upper Room. Despite
being paralysed by fear and doubt, they are still together. Into

their midst Jesus offers the gift of peace. 'It is not a matter of mysteriously passing through locked doors of a *room*, but of prayerfully opening the locked doors of our *hearts*, that allows the community to perceive the presence of the Risen One.'[7]

Jesus identifies himself by showing his wounded hands and side (v. 20). These are the hands into which God has given all things (3:35; 13:3). In the midst of the disciples' fear, and against the impending violence of both Jews and Romans, the meaningful gift of peace is offered. Jesus' appearance and his peace giving do not mark the end of discipleship, but rather its true beginning. 'As the Father sent me, so am I sending you' (v. 21). 'The divine authority that Jesus has been given is *totally transferred to the community*.'[8]

The community's new authority brings a shared relationship with the Holy Spirit (v. 22). The new relationship brings new responsibilities and Jesus gives some practical advice about forgiveness in community: 'If you let go of someone's sins, they are forgiven; if you hold on to them, they are retained' (v. 23). Given the community's previous failures and imperfections, together with the potential for recrimination and bearing grudges, strategies for forgiveness are essential to build up community. A community claiming to be a bearer of 'good news for all people' is seen as hypocritical if fear, guilt and an unforgiving spirit govern its life.

Talking Points

Locked doors provide security of a sort for fearful people, but they limit action. Jesus' purpose in seeking to overcome the disciples' doubt and fear was to open the doors in order to confront the world with his truth. Where are the locked doors, the places of fear in the church, in our communities today? How relevant is Jesus' advice about 'letting go' of grudges, failures and imperfections? Why is this so difficult?

Reflection and Action
This week the Reflection and Action is quite personal, and
does not require any sharing with the group. In what ways do
you practise forgiveness? Are there people you find it hard to
forgive? During this week, reflect on the way you both 'forgive'
and 'retain' the faults of others. Ask God to help you make an
act of forgiveness towards someone whose sin you have
retained. How will you demonstrate that forgiveness?

Worship
Offer your act of worship as suggested for **Easter Day**.

For next time, the **worship convenor** should arrange for
someone to bring a roll or pitta bread. Two people should
prepare a short litany with the response, 'If you forgive anyone's sins, they are forgiven.' After the litany, let someone
break a piece of bread and give it to their neighbour saying,
'Your sins are forgiven.' Each should then offer bread to the
neighbour saying the same words. The worship convenor
should conclude the worship with the words:

'Do not be unbelieving any more, but believe.'

The Second Sunday after Easter

Getting started
Begin with the act of worship the group has prepared. Include
today's reading in your worship.

Read Luke 24:13–35.
(Other readings: Isaiah 25:6–9; Revelation 19:6–9.)

13 Now that very same day, two of them were on their way to a
14 village called Emmaus, seven miles from Jerusalem, and they
15 were talking together about all that had happened. And it
     happened that as they were walking together and discussing
16 it, Jesus himself came up and walked by their side; but their
17 eyes were prevented from recognising him. He said to them,

'What are all these things that you are discussing as you walk
along?' They stopped, their faces downcast.

18   Then one of them, called Cleopas, answered him, 'You
must be the only person staying in Jerusalem who does not
know the things that have been happening there these last
19   few days.' He asked, 'What things?' They answered, 'All about
Jesus of Nazareth, who showed himself a prophet powerful
20   in action and speech before God and the whole people; and
how our chief priests and our leaders handed him over to be
21   sentenced to death, and had him crucified. Our own hope
had been that he would be the one to set Israel free. And
this is not all: two whole days have now gone by since it all
22   happened; and some women from our group have astounded
23   us: they went to the tomb in the early morning, and when
they could not find the body, they came back to tell us they
24   had seen a vision of angels who declared he was alive. Some
of our friends went to the tomb and found everything exactly
as the women had reported, but of him they saw nothing.'

25   Then he said to them, 'You foolish men! So slow to believe
26   all that the prophets have said! Was it not necessary that the
27   Christ should suffer before entering into his glory?' Then
starting with Moses and going through all the prophets, he
explained to them the passages throughout the scriptures that
were about himself.

28   When they drew near to the village to which they were
29   going, he made as if to go on; but they pressed him to stay
with them saying, 'It is nearly evening, and the day is almost
30   over.' So he went in to stay with them. Now while he was
with them at table, he took the bread and said the blessing;
31   then he broke it and handed it to them. And their eyes were
opened and they recognised him; but he had vanished from
32   their sight. Then they said to each other, 'Did not our hearts
burn within us as he talked to us on the road and explained
the scriptures to us?'

33   They set out that instant and returned to Jerusalem. There
they found the Eleven assembled together with their com-

34   panions, who said to them, 'The Lord has indeed risen and
35   has appeared to Simon.' Then they told their story of what
     had happened on the road and how they had recognised him
     at the breaking of bread.

Comment

This is a story about going back to the beginning. The account
begins with the two disciples leaving Jerusalem, and ends with
them making the return journey on the same day. The events
of the crucifixion and the rumours of the empty tomb leave
them questioning, 'What's it all about?'

They return several hours later with a story and fresh hope.
The late night walk along a road notorious for muggers brought
them into conversation with a 'stranger'. He quickly turns their
question, 'What is going on here?' into a statement: 'If you
want to know what is going on now, you have to know what
went on before.'

If you want to understand the present you must understand
the past. 'If you want to know what it means to be a Jew, you'll
have to reflect on what it meant to be a Jew in Moses' time, in
Isaiah's time, in Jeremiah's time.'[9]

So what did it mean? Simply, to have a vision of a new path,
a new people, living lives of reconciliation and justice, bearing
each other's burdens, being compassionate. The 'stranger' is
offered hospitality. The 'stranger' becomes a companion
(literally cum-panis – with bread). Words have been turned
into action, but it is only the beginning, for as the companion
appears, so he disappears. The disciples are left with a new
understanding, a vision and a task. They return to the centre
of the struggle, Jerusalem. It is still the same place: danger
lurks, their compatriots are hiding out; but now they are ready
to take on the world whatever the cost.

Talking Points

Can you recall any experience in which new understanding
gave you energy to face a particular challenge? Has any

'stranger' ever given you an unexpected insight into something important in your life? The external circumstances had not changed for Jesus' followers, their own lives were still at risk. How close is the experience of the disciples to yours on your day-by-day Christian journey?

Reflection and Action
If we are to change things, we need to understand the way things are. Beginning with your group, church and then the wider community, ask: What are the situations that need healing, reconciliation, justice and compassion? Whose burden needs bearing? What doors need unlocking? What small steps can you plan to bring about some change?

Worship
Plan to have an informal supper together next week. The convenor should encourage everyone to bring a simple dish of food to share. Ask half the group to choose a grace, a prayer of thanks for food. Ask the other half of the group to offer prayers for 'strangers', 'healing', 'justice' and 'compassion'. At the beginning of the meal, ask someone to read John 21:1–14; then have half the group offer their grace; ask the remainder to offer their prayers to close the meal.

The Third Sunday after Easter

Getting started
Share a common meal and worship as suggested last time.

Read John 21:1–14.
(Other readings: Isaiah 61:1–7; 1 Corinthians 15:1–11.)

1   Later on, Jesus revealed himself again to the disciples. It was
2   by the Sea of Tiberias, and it happened like this: Simon Peter, Thomas called the Twin, Nathanael from Cana in Galilee, the sons of Zebedee and two more of his disciples were
3   together. Simon Peter said, 'I'm going fishing.' They replied,

'We'll come with you.' They went out and got into the boat
but caught nothing that night.

4   When it was already light, there stood Jesus on the shore,
5   though the disciples did not realise that it was Jesus. Jesus
       called out, 'Haven't you caught anything, friends?' And when
6   they answered, 'No,' he said, 'Throw the net out to starboard
       and you'll find something.' So they threw the net out and
7   could not haul it in because of the quantity of fish. The
       disciple whom Jesus loved said to Peter, 'It is the Lord.' At
       these words, 'It is the Lord,' Simon Peter tied his outer
       garment round him (for he had nothing on) and jumped into
8   the water. The other disciples came on in the boat, towing the
       net with fish; they were only about a hundred yards from
       land.

9   As soon as they came ashore they saw that there was some
10   bread there and a charcoal fire with fish cooking on it. Jesus
11   said, 'Bring some of the fish you have just caught.' Simon
       Peter went aboard and dragged the net ashore, full of big
       fish, one hundred and fifty-three of them; and in spite of
12   there being so many the net was not broken. Jesus said,
       'Come and have breakfast.' None of the disciples was bold
       enough to ask, 'Who are you?' They knew quite well it was
13   the Lord. Jesus then stepped forward, took the bread and
14   gave it to them, and the same with the fish. This was the third
       time that Jesus revealed himself to the disciples after rising
       from the dead.

Comment

The guests on this fishing trip all have one trait in common.

They have each revealed their doubts about their relationship with Jesus: Peter, by his denial; Thomas, by his
demand for physical proof; and Nathaniel, by his doubt
that 'good' could come out of Nazareth. At the same time,
each has also offered an explicit confession of faith: Peter,
of Jesus as the 'Holy One of God' (6:69); Thomas, 'My

Lord and my God' (20:28); and Nathaniel, 'You are the
Son of God, the king of Israel' (1:49). Finally, each has his
'confession' followed by a rhetorical question by Jesus that
expressed his own doubts about the depth of the disciples'
commitment (6:70; 20:29; 1:50).[10]

In the story of the breakfast, the disciples are on the point of
returning to their old ways. It is safe, economically secure and
away from the limelight. John was writing his Gospel for a
community of people under suspicion and fear of arrest and
trial from hostile Roman authorities. With this ever-present
danger of arrest and, worse, anonymity, a return to 'business
as usual' must have been appealing.

Two clairvoyant happenings occur; first, the 'miracle' of the
full fishing net, recalling earlier times and the distant promise
to become 'fishers of people'. Second, the bread and the fish
breakfast recalling the feeding of the hungry five thousand.
Both events remind the disciples of the mission of God. Peter
might have noticed that the last time he stood by a fire, it was
to deny Jesus; now the warmth of the same kind of fire beckons
him back into a new relationship. It seems to give him superhuman strength, for he alone brings the fishing net up the
beach! (v. 11)

Talking Points
Do you have people with whom you can share your doubts?
When have you felt like giving up? Have there been any experiences which have recalled you to your faith and prevented you
from returning to 'business as usual'?

Reflection and Action
Share any small steps you have made this week to bring about
change. As you look at the situations in your group, church or
neighbourhood that seem to need change, how will you make
sure you don't just give up when things look risky, or your own
comfort is threatened? Have you been able to decide on any

group activity you might engage in to help make change possible?

Worship
The **worship convenor** should find the words of Sydney Carter's hymn, 'When I needed a neighbour, were you there?' Provide copies for people next time. Two people should prepare some prayers, making the focus your community group and neighbourhood.

Fourth Sunday after Easter

Getting started
Begin with singing 'When I needed a neighbour'. Briefly share your own experiences of 'needing a neighbour' during the past week. Before you discuss John 21, offer the prayers for the group and neighbourhood.

Read John 21:15–22.
(Other readings: Isaiah 62:1–5; Revelation 3:14–end.)

15   **When they had eaten, Jesus said to Simon Peter, 'Simon son of John, do you love me more than these others do?' He answered, 'Yes, Lord, you know I love you.' Jesus said to**
16   **him, 'Feed my lambs.' A second time he said to him, 'Simon son of John, do you love me?' He replied, 'Yes, Lord, you know I love you.' Jesus said to him, 'Look after my sheep.'**
17   **Then he said to him a third time, 'Simon son of John, do you love me?' Peter was hurt that he asked him a third time, 'Do you love me?' and said, 'Lord, you know everything; you know I love you.' Jesus said to him, 'Feed my sheep.**

18   **In all truth I tell you,**
              when you were young
              you put on your belt
              and walked where you liked;
              but when you grow old

> you will stretch out your hands,
> and somebody else will put a belt round you
> and take you where you would rather not go.'

19 In these words he indicated the kind of death by which Peter would give glory to God. After this he said, 'Follow me.'

20 Peter turned and saw the disciple whom Jesus loved following them – the one who had leant back close to his chest at the supper and had said to him, 'Lord, who is it that will

21 betray you?' Seeing him, Peter said to Jesus, 'What about

22 him, Lord?' Jesus answered, 'If I want him to stay behind till I come, what does it matter to you? You are to follow me.'

Comment

There is something of a tussle between traditions in the Church going on here. The Gospel of John is written for a sect-like tradition within the Church. They were basically suspicious of the more hierarchical, patriarchal Church represented by Peter, Paul and other apostles. Yet danger exists for both 'Churches' and they are both threatened with persecution, and ultimately extinction. Certainly members of both groups experienced martyrdom. The call at the Last Supper for people to 'love one another' (15:17), and as Jesus loved them (15:12), is critical for the future mission.

The narrator is anxious that both traditions value each other. He shows Jesus revealing to Peter and to John their respective vocations. Peter is to follow Jesus to a martyr's death, by crucifixion. John, on the other hand, is called to remain, to be witness.

It was widely thought that martyrdom was the highest calling, and paradoxically it often happens to the most unlikely people, the ones with a record of cowardice or unfaithfulness. But perhaps what is most important here is that Peter, who represents the more hierarchical Church, is to suffer martyrdom, whereas the more charismatic Church leader, John, is called to remain.

Jesus, however, is not into competition (21:22). Each to his calling – 'Peter is to incarnate the laying down of life, the Beloved Disciple will model remaining in Jesus' love.'[11] Remaining, living faithfully, and bearing fruit that lasts is a more common, but no less costly calling. The day-by-day struggle of redressing injustice, working for the coming of God's new order, saps and drains life and energy.

Bearing witness is not a soft option to martyrdom – just its counterpart.

Talking Points

This account is a very ordinary story of breakfast by a lake and a conversation between people who know each other well. It is full of the usual range of human emotions and attitudes, including guilt, jealousy, the desire for acceptance and the hope that faith in Jesus is a worthwhile life investment.

Where does this story touch your story? How can we make more effective our own calling of remaining and bearing witness? What might this mean in our situation? Are there any lessons here for the different Churches today in our country? What are they?

Reflection and Action

St Anthony was once asked, 'What must one do in order to please God?' The old man replied, 'Pay attention to what I tell you: whoever you may be, always have God before your eyes; whatever you do, do it according to the testimony of the Holy Scriptures; in whatever place you live do not easily leave it. Keep these precepts and you will be saved.'[12]

How do these words of St Anthony and the reading from St John give you a direction for the work in your community?

Worship – for next week:

Prayer has been described as: 'rattling God's cage and waking God up and setting God free and giving this famished God water and this starved God food and cutting the ropes off

God's hands and the manacles off God's feet and washing the caked sweat from God's eyes and then watching God swell with life vitality and energy and following God wherever God goes.'[13] How do you want to rattle God's cage?

Use your imagination and have a really good rant!

The Fifth Sunday after Easter

Getting started
If you could ask God a single question, what would it be?

Read John 16:24-end.
(Other readings: Hosea 6:1–6; 1 Corinthians 15:21–8.)

24   'Until now you have not asked anything in my name.
       Ask and you will receive,
       and so your joy may be complete.
25   I have been telling you these things in veiled language.
       The hour is coming
       when I shall no longer speak to you in veiled language
       but tell you about the Father in plain words.
26   When that day comes
       you will ask in my name;
       and I do not say that I shall pray to the Father for you,
27   because the Father himself loves you
       for loving me,
       and believing that I came from God.
28   I came from the Father and have come into the world
       and now I am leaving the world to go to the Father.'

29   His disciples said, 'Now you are speaking plainly and not
30   using veiled language. Now we see that you know everything
       and need not wait for questions to be put into words; because
31   of this we believe you came from God.' Jesus answered them:

               Do you believe at last?
32   Listen, the time will come – indeed it has come already –

> **when you are going to be scattered, each going his own way**
> **and leaving me alone.**
> **And yet I am not alone,**
> **because the Father is with me.**

33   **I have told you all this**
> **so that you may find peace in me.**
> **In the world you will have hardship,**
> **but be courageous:**
> **I have conquered the world.**

Comment

In Jewish tradition, God was never referred to by name. It was believed to be over-familiar. Jesus observes that the disciples have never asked him for anything by name (v. 24). In fact, notes one writer, the disciples haven't called Jesus anything other than 'Lord' in the Gospel of John so far except on one occasion (1:45). 'Indeed this attitude has persisted throughout the centuries, as evidenced by the pious seeking of the mediation of Mary and the saints that has arisen because of the fear of asking directly in the name of Jesus.'[14]

Jesus emphasises his desire for the intimacy of friendship (v. 26), and he says this is what the Father also wants (v. 27). Jesus calls them 'friends' (15:15) and he describes the Father as being 'friends' with Jesus; and 'friends' with them because they have been friendly with him, 'believing that I came from God' (v. 27). If the disciples and the Father are friends, he argues, a time will come when Jesus will not need to act as intermediary and interpreter, but anyone can 'ask the Father in my name'.

Jesus does not make rash statements – he is 'truth' (14:6) and 'tells the truth' (16:7), even when the truth is unpalatable (15:18–20). There are no guarantees in following Jesus, except facing 'hardship' (16:33) and 'finding peace' in Jesus (v. 33). These words are the last Jesus spoke directly to the disciples before his crucifixion. They are an invitation to stop being fearful and become 'courageous' (v. 33). They are called to a 'kind of living in which friendship and love replace violence and lies. It is a difficult road between here and there, as anyone who has taken the first steps knows all too well.'[15]

Talking Points
This section of *Seeds of the Word* finishes at this point. The purpose of these reflections on Jesus' resurrection appearances has been to help us to face the difficulty disciples have following Jesus, and how important it is to be realistic about the challenge. When we ask, as the disciples often did, 'What's it all about?', our small faith communities need to be places of love, hope and encouragement. To be places of hope, forgiveness has to be practised, fear and guilt overcome, strangers welcomed, in justice redressed, witness maintained.

Reflection and Action
Make some assessment of how you as a group feel you are doing. Decide together whether you want to continue meeting, and when.

Celebration
Whether you continue to meet as a group or not, plan a picnic or barbecue to celebrate your life together during these past weeks.

ASCENSION, PENTECOST AND TRINITY

Ascension marks an end and a beginning. Advent and Lent are seasons of preparation. Easter marks a celebration of hope. Ascension provides a climax to a series of events that have been cataclysmic and mysterious for Jesus and his community.

Arrest, trial, crucifixion, burial – events traumatic enough in themselves, but on top of these come the mysteries of resurrection and ascension marking the end of the earthly encounter of Jesus with his followers.

Ascension heralds the beginning of discipleship practice in the world. It is a time of promise. A promise for all human beings who seek to overcome evil with good. Jesus said, 'Anyone who proves victorious I will allow to share my throne, just as I have myself overcome and have taken my seat with my Father on his throne' (Revelation 3:21).

Pentecost, the Jewish festival of the first fruits of the harvest, follows the Ascension. For the disciples of Jesus, it was to be the moment of empowering by the Holy Spirit.

In the Common Lectionary there are some twenty-two Sundays that follow **Pentecost**. In *Seeds of the Word* these are grouped into units to give people as much flexibility for using the material as possible (see pages 138–214). A short series begins this season marking the events of:

Ascension
Pentecost
The Trinity

Basic Preparation

As you begin *Seeds of the Word* for **Ascension, Pentecost and Trinity**, don't forget to reread pages 23–7. Agree **why, where** and **how** you are meeting; also decide on the allocation of **ministries**.

The Liturgical Colours for this season are **white** for Ascension and Trinity; **red** for Pentecost Sunday; **green** for the Sundays after Pentecost.

Creating a Focus

There is a lot of dreaming going on in the readings over the next few weeks! North American Indians used to hang a 'dream catcher' in their tepees. Good dreams were caught and held in the centre; bad dreams trailed from the threads. As you work through the various units in Pentecost, try and reflect some of your hopes and dreams for the future in the focus you create, as you seek to build up faith, hope and love together in Jesus Christ.

Seasonal Collects:

> **Almighty God,**
> **as we believe your only-begotten Son our Lord**
>   **Jesus Christ**
> **to have ascended into the heavens,**
> **so may we also in heart and mind thither ascend**
> **and with him continually dwell;**
> **who is alive and reigns with you and the Holy**
>   **Spirit,**
> **one God, now and for ever.**

> **Almighty God,**
> **who on the day of Pentecost**
> **sent your Holy Spirit to the disciples**
> **with the wind from heaven and in tongues**
>   **of flame,**
> **filling them with joy**
>   **and boldness to preach the gospel:**
> **send us out in the power of the same Spirit**
> **to witness to your truth**
> **and to draw all people to the fire of your love:**
> **through Jesus Christ our Lord. Amen.**

> **Almighty and eternal God,**
> **you have revealed yourself**
>   **as Father, Son, and Holy Spirit,**
> **and live and reign in the perfect unity of love.**
> **Hold us firm in this faith,**
> **that we may know you in all your ways**
> **and evermore rejoice in your eternal glory,**
> **who are three Persons in one God,**
> **now and for ever. Amen.**[1]

Ascension Day

Getting started:

What is your most recurrent or memorable dream? Do you write your dreams down? Do you think you have ever been helped by a dream? How?

Read Daniel 7:1–14.

(Other readings: Acts 1:1–11; Matthew 28:16-end.)

1   In the first year of Belshazzar king of Babylon, Daniel had a dream and visions that passed through his head as he lay in bed. He wrote the dream down and this is how the narrative
2   began: Daniel said, 'I have been seeing visions in the night. I saw that the four winds of heaven were stirring up the Great
3   Sea; four great beasts emerged from the sea, each different
4   from the others. The first was like a lion with eagle's wings and, as I looked, its wings were torn off, and it was lifted off the ground and set standing on its feet like a human; and it
5   was given a human heart. And there before me was a second beast, like a bear, rearing up on one side, with three ribs in its mouth, between its teeth. "Up!" came the command. "Eat
6   quantities of flesh!" After this I looked; and there before me was another beast, like a leopard, and with four bird's wings on its flanks; it had four heads and was granted authority.
7   Next in the visions of the night, I saw another vision: there before me was a fourth beast, fearful, terrifying, very strong; it had great iron teeth, and ate its victims, crushed them, and trampled their remains underfoot. It was different from the previous beasts and had ten horns.
8   'While I was looking at these horns I saw another horn sprouting among them, a little one; three of the original horns were pulled out by the roots to make way for it; and in this horn I saw eyes like human eyes, and a mouth full of boasting.

9   While I was watching,
           thrones were set in place,

and one most venerable took his seat.
His robe was white as snow,
the hair of his head as pure as wool.
His throne was a blaze of flames,
its wheels were a burning fire.

10   A stream of fire poured out,
issuing from his presence.
A thousand thousand waited on him,
ten thousand times ten thousand stood before him.
The court was in session
and the books lay open.

11 'I went on watching: then, because of the noise made by the boastings of the horn, as I watched, the beast was put to death, and its body destroyed and committed to the flames.

12 The other beasts were deprived of their empire, but received a lease of life for a season and a time.

13   I was gazing into the visions of the night
when I saw, coming on the clouds of heaven,
as it were a son of man.
He came to the One most venerable
and was led into his presence.

14   On him was conferred rule,
honour and kingship
and all peoples, nations and languages
   became his servants.
His rule is an everlasting rule
which will never pass away,
and his kingship will never come to an end.'

Comment

Dreams and visions are often the way that Bible writers deal with mystery. Hidden things that are about to be revealed are frequently expressed through dreams. The word 'apocalypse' means 'making known what used to be secret'. Daniel's vision is like that. He sees himself appearing in court, giving evidence about the earth's oppressive, destructive rulers and powers (vv. 1–8). Everything looks hopeless. Oppression, fear, terror continue unchecked (vv. 7–8). New oppressors, like horns, grow before his eyes (v. 8).

Suddenly, at the moment of apparently unchecked evil, something dramatic happens. Furniture removers arrive (well, dreams are like that!) and put into place a set of thrones. A judge appears (v. 9) and evidence is presented (v. 10). Judgement begins. The Beast is judged (v. 11) and power begins to ebb from other nations (v. 12).

Now clouds come into view (v. 13) and the son of man, the Human One, appears. This is the one who has vanquished the powers of oppression, fear and terror, and upon him is conferred honour and kingship (v. 14).

Jesus, in Mark's Gospel, prefers the title 'son of man', 'the Human One', to 'Messiah' or 'Son of God'. At his trial (Mark 14:53–65), at the moment of apparent hopelessness, Jesus, using the words of Daniel (Daniel 7:13; Mark 14:62), reveals the secret: 'I am . . . the Son of man, seated at the right hand of the Power and coming with the clouds of heaven.'

'The powers have had their day. The myth of the Human One overthrowing the rulers of the age is a revolutionary one that legitimises resistance to the dominant order, and promises its demise.'[2] The authorities will shortly witness the end of the old order. To them it will appear that they are the victors, but when 'the sun darkens and the sanctuary curtain is rent in two (the political symbol), the world order has been overthrown and the powers have fallen.'[3]

The Ascension lays down a challenge for discipleship. Will we 'stand here looking into the sky?' (Acts 1:11), or be ashamed of the Human One 'in this sinful and adulterous generation' (Mark 8:38)? Or will we resist the dominant order where it resists the rule of God? The Ascension provides the hope that whatever is suffered for the sake of right will not be in vain – the ascended Christ is King!

Talking Points

Where is hopelessness, terror and fear going unchecked at this time? Where do you see the dominant order needing to be resisted? Can you identify any particular incident that made you feel hopeless and powerless? Do you see any signs of where Christ is Lord of the Powers?

Reflection and Action

Identify a situation in which you feel helpless. It might be a local situation or a 'prisoner of conscience', a famine, a suffering child, etc. Ask the question 'why?' – 'Why do we feel helpless?' You might reply, 'Because the problem seems so big.' Ask again, 'But why?' – 'There are too many difficulties.' 'But why?' Keep asking the question, 'But why?' until you reach a point where you can make some small step to change things. What action will you take? Decide who is going to do what, and report progress at your next meeting.

Worship

Ask people to close their eyes. Have someone read Daniel 7:9–10. Let people be silent for a few minutes, allowing themselves to imagine the picture in Daniel's dream.

Ask someone else to read Daniel 7:13–14.

Then say together:

> Christ our lover
> to whom we try to cling;
> as you have reached into our depths
> and drawn us to love you,
> so make us open, freely to let you go;
> that you may return in unexpected power
> to change the world through us
> in your name. Amen.[4]

For next time ask each member of the group to recall a person, or text, or hymn that has at some time or another been an encouragement to them. Share your encouragements, and the **worship convenor** should ask someone to prepare one or two prayers of encouragement.

Sunday after Ascension

Getting started
Begin with the time of worship as outlined last week.

Read Ephesians 1:15-end.
(Other readings: Daniel 7:9–14; Luke 24:45-end.)

15 That is why I, having once heard about your faith in the Lord Jesus, and your love for all God's holy people, have never
16 failed to thank God for you and to remember you in my
17 prayers. May the God of our Lord Jesus Christ, the Father of glory, give you a spirit of wisdom and perception of what
18 is revealed, to bring you to full knowledge of him. May he enlighten the eyes of your mind, so that you can see what hope his call holds for you, how rich is the glory of the
19 heritage he offers among his holy people, and how extraordinarily great is the power that he has exercised for us as
20 believers; this accords with the strength of his power at work in Christ, the power he exercised in raising him from the
21 dead and enthroning him at his right hand, in heaven, far above every principality, ruling force, power or sovereignty, or any other name that can be named, not only in this age,
22 but also in the age to come. He has put all things under his
23 feet, and made him, as he is above all things, the head of the Church; which is his Body, the fullness of him who is filled, all in all.

Comment

We all need encouragement in our faith (v. 15). It is good to have others praying for us, particularly when times are difficult, and it is hard to see God at work in the world. The readers of the letter to the Ephesians would have had as much difficulty as people do today believing that evil had been conquered by

Christ on the cross. But that is the staggering claim of this letter.

Like us, the Ephesians would have witnessed, as we do,

> Sincere attempts of politicians and kings, sales clerks and business people to create a world of justice and morality, to abolish inhuman practices, even to give correct change. But they have to struggle to do so against almost insuperable odds. The fact is the Powers are as powerful as ever, as no people should know better than we who have survived into the grim twilight of the twentieth century since the crucifixion.[5]

It is an act of faith to believe that Christ is in charge of 'every principality, ruling force, power or sovereignty' (v. 21) and that 'God has put all things under his feet' (v. 22). Significant evidence seems almost totally non-existent.

Most modern Christians see religion as a personal relationship with a personal God. The writer of Ephesians sees heaven (where God dwells) in a continuous struggle with what is evil, short-sighted and ignorant on earth. The struggle is pictured as continuing until God's victory brings in 'a new heaven and a new earth' (Revelation 21:1). Christians are expected to join this struggle. 'Just as peasants liberated from the control of military dictatorship are not freed from conflict but freed *for* conflict, the Christian is recruited to the grace-full struggle to bring the world to the truth (1:13) that the crucified and risen Christ is its principle of harmony and power' (1:20–3).[6] To be freed for conflict, we need the mutual support and comfort of others in prayer and community, or fellowship.

Talking Points
Who has encouraged you this week? To whom have you offered encouragement? Who do you think is making a sincere attempt to create justice and morality and abolish inhuman practices? Can you offer any encouragement to them? How do you feel about joining 'the struggle to bring the world to the truth'?

Reflection and Action
How did the action you planned last week work out? Have you anything to **celebrate?** How will you do that? What action plan has emerged from your discussion today? Are there people you have identified who need encouragement and prayer? Who? What will you do now?

Worship
Symbols are often helpful in worship. Next week marks the celebration of the giving of the Spirit at Pentecost. Choose a symbol of what Pentecost means for you. Bring and share your symbol with the group. The **worship convenor** should ask someone to choose a song or hymn to sing together, such as *Veni Sancti Spiritus* from the Taizé songs. Prepare some prayers with the response:

LEADER: The Lord declares,
PEOPLE: I shall pour out my Spirit on all humanity.

Pentecost

Getting started
What is the most courageous thing you have ever done? Where do you sense the courage came from?

Read Acts 2:1–21.
(Other readings: Genesis 11:1–9; John 20:19–23.)

1　When Pentecost day came round, they had all met together,
2　when suddenly there came from heaven a sound as of a violent wind which filled the entire house in which they were
3　sitting; and there appeared to them tongues as of fire; these separated and came to rest on the head of each of them.
4　They were all filled with the Holy Spirit and began to speak in different languages as the Spirit gave them power to express themselves.
5　　Now there were devout men living in Jerusalem from every

6   nation under heaven, and at this sound they all assembled,
    and each one was bewildered to hear these men speaking his
7   own language. They were amazed and astonished. 'Surely,'
8   they said, 'all these men speaking are Galileans? How does it
9   happen that each of us hears them in his own native language?
10 Parthians, Medes and Elamites; people from Mesopotamia,
    Judaea and Cappadocia, Pontus and Asia, Phrygia and Pam-
    phylia, Egypt and the parts of Libya round Cyrene; residents
11 of Rome – Jews and proselytes alike – Cretans and Arabs,
12 we hear them preaching in our own language about the mar-
13 vels of God.' Everyone was amazed and perplexed; they asked
    one another what it all meant. Some, however, laughed it off.
14 'They have been drinking too much new wine,' they said.

        Then Peter stood up with the Eleven and addressed them
    in a loud voice:

        'Men of Judaea, and all you who live in Jerusalem, make
15 no mistake about this but listen carefully to what I say. These
    men are not drunk, as you imagine; why it is only the third
16 hour of the day. On the contrary, this is what the prophet
    was saying:

17   In the last days – the Lord declares –
            I shall pour out my Spirit on all humanity.
            Your sons and daughters shall prophesy,
            your young people shall see visions,
            your old people dream dreams.
18   Even on the slaves, men and women,
            shall I pour out my Spirit.
19   I will show portents in the sky above
            and signs on the earth below.
20   The sun will be turned into darkness
            and the moon into blood
            before the day of the Lord comes,
            that great and terrible Day.
21   And all who call on the name of the Lord will be saved.'

Comment

Albert Camus, a French philosopher addressing a group of Christians in 1948, spoke of his yearning and complaint. As the preparations for war were made, he observed that victims grew, fear spread, and the Church remained 'unconscionably silent', or spoke unconvincingly.

Camus was candid and blunt:

> For a long time during those frightful years I waited for a great voice in the Church. I, an unbeliever? Precisely. For I knew that the spirit would be lost if it did not utter a cry of condemnation when faced with force ... What the world expects of Christians is that Christians should speak out loud and clear, and that they should voice their condemnation in such a way that never a doubt, never a slightest doubt, could arise in the heart of the simplest person. That they should get away from abstraction and confront the bloodstained face history has taken on today. The grouping we need is a group of people resolved to speak out clearly and to pay up personally.[7]

At Pentecost the early Christian community faced a stark choice. Would they be ruled by fear, staying silent, confined to their hiding place? They knew the score. Jesus had been executed for his commitment to the justice of God (Matthew 6:33). The Roman and Jewish authorities were jittery. Jesus had prophesied, ' ... Strike the shepherd and the sheep of the flock will be scattered' (Matthew 26:31).

The boldness and freedom with which Peter spoke (v. 14) was more indicative of a free-thinking democracy than a police state. His call to people 'to save themselves from this crooked generation' (2:40) was both individual and corporate (all the nations of the earth were represented in Jerusalem, vv. 9–11). Those listening would have been aware of the political pressure of the watching authorities. Making a response to Peter's message was to choose an allegiance that risked conflict and confrontation, regardless of what it offered of freedom and hope. If you read the Gospel references to the promise of the Spirit (Luke 12:11–12; Matthew 10:17–20; Mark 13:9–10; John 15) you will see that each reveals the conflict, controversy and persecution resulting from taking a public stand.

Talking Points
Do you feel Albert Camus' words are relevant now? How? Do you think the world expects Christians, and other people of faith, to speak out loud against the bloodstained face history has taken on today? In recent years, many Christians have chosen Pentecost as an occasion for protest and witness. Do you believe this is an appropriate way of celebrating this festival? What are the issues you feel strongly about? How do you express this?

Reflection and Action
How will you as a group **celebrate** Pentecost? Has anything in today's study helped you to decide on particular action about the issues over which you feel strongly? Are there people who need your support in their stand for justice? How will you offer support?

Worship
Next week ask someone to bring a world map and some candles, and each person should bring newspaper cuttings which reflect concerns you have as a group. Use these items to create an act of worship reflecting your concerns.

Trinity Sunday

Getting started
Begin with an act of worship, using the map, candles and newspaper cuttings.

Read Isaiah 6:1–8.
(Other readings: Ephesians 1:3–14; John 14:8–19.)

1   In the year of King Uzziah's death I saw the Lord seated on
2   a high and lofty throne; his train filled the sanctuary. Above
     him stood seraphs, each one with six wings: two to cover its
3   face, two to cover its feet and two for flying; and they were
     shouting these words to each other:

> Holy, holy, holy is the Lord Sabaoth.
> His glory fills the whole earth.

4   The door-posts shook at the sound of their shouting, and
5   the Temple was full of smoke. Then I said:

> 'Woe is me! I am lost,
> for I am a man of unclean lips
> and I live among a people of unclean lips,
> and my eyes have seen the King, the Lord Sabaoth.'

6   Then one of the seraphs flew to me, holding in its hand a
     live coal which it had taken from the altar with a pair of
7   tongs. With this it touched my mouth and said:

> 'Look, this has touched your lips,
> your guilt has been removed
> and your sin forgiven.'

8   I then heard the voice of the Lord saying:

> 'Whom shall I send? Who will go for us?'

> And I said, 'Here am I, send me.'

Comment

Dreaming in church is usually done by the congregation, rather
than the priest! But Isaiah, in the midst of the evening sacrifice
in the Temple, is distracted. He has good reason. Politically,
things are difficult. King Uzziah (one of the better monarchs)
has died of leprosy. Once again the storm clouds of war are
gathering round the tiny state of Judah. Who should it seek to

ally itself with – Assyria or Egypt? Uncertainty was
everywhere.

Suddenly Isaiah is transported in a vision. No ordinary one
either. He reported later, 'I saw the Lord on a high and lofty
throne' (v. 1). This Lord is the Lord Sabaoth (the Lord of
armies). 'Whom shall I send?' asks the Lord, who is seeking
allies in the struggle for justice. Isaiah knows he is implicated
in the sins of his people who have become indifferent to their
faith, ceased to practise justice, and sought allies whose sole
objective is empire building. This dream marks a moment of
judgement. Isaiah is lifted from the floor; a burning coal
touches his lips (vv. 6–7), his sin is forgiven, his lips are free to
speak, and to respond to God's plea for allies: 'Here am I,
send me' (v. 9).

The message is not comfortable (that'll teach him to dream
in church!). 'God's people had forgotten their call to be a holy
nation. No longer were they living in holy non-conformity,
trusting in God to protect and provide. Instead, their lifestyle
had become one of unholy conformity to the patterns of life
of the surrounding nations.'[8]

This call is to a specific mission; Isaiah is to address the
political leaders of his time, and unfold God's historical plan
(Isaiah 7 and 8). Isaiah subsequently warns King Ahaz
(Uzziah's son and heir) that God says, 'If you will not take
your stand on me you will not stand firm' (7:9).

Isaiah was awestruck by his vision of God's holiness and it
led him into mission. St Paul understood God's purpose many
centuries later and expressed it like this: when the time is right,
God will 'bring everything together under Christ . . . everything
in the heavens and everything on earth' (Ephesians 1:10). The
invitation of God is to be like Jesus and to be 'stamped with
the seal of the Holy Spirit of the Promise' (Ephesians 1:13).

Talking Points

Have you ever sensed the presence of God? What was it like?
Did you feel that God wanted a particular response from you?

Who are the prophets of our times? What are they saying?
How are their voices being heard?

Reflection and Action

In what ways during the past few weeks have you seen a vision
of something you ought to do? What is it? Prepare yourselves
with an act of penitence, recognising like Isaiah, that we are
people 'of unclean lips', implicated in the sins of our community and nation.

Afterwards plan a **celebration** for your life together during
these past few weeks, and decide how you are going to take
things from here. Why not look for a way of sharing your group
experience more widely in your church?

THE PENTECOST SEASON

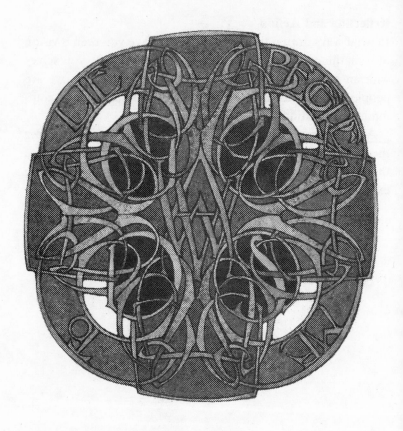

In the northern hemisphere the **Pentecost** season occurs during the time for sowing, growing and harvesting. **The Liturgical Colour** for this time in the Church's year is **green**. Green symbolises lushness and growth. The twenty-three Sundays in this season are designed to be a time of sowing, growing and harvesting the seeds of faith. It is a time for learning and experimenting with the faith.

For many users of *Seeds of the Word* there will be time for vacation during the next few weeks. *Seeds of the Word* in the next few months is divided into different length units. You may want to choose a unit for three, four or six meetings. Look at the following menu and decide which will be helpful to you as a group in your community building in the next few months:

Unit 1   *Being the People of God*   *(Pentecost 2)*
              Being Friends of God   *(Pentecost 3)*
              Being Free for God   *(Pentecost 4)*

This unit is based on John 15 and a community model of Church.

Unit 2   *New Law*   *(Pentecost 5)*
              New Humanity   *(Pentecost 6)*
              New Way   *(Pentecost 7)*
              New Fruit   *(Pentecost 8)*
              New Resources   *(Pentecost 9)*
              New Mind   *(Pentecost 10)*

Unit 3   *The Serving Community*   *(Pentecost 11)*
              The Witnessing Community   *(Pentecost 12)*
              The Suffering Community   *(Pentecost 13)*

Unit 4   *Family*   *(Pentecost 14)*
              Society   *(Pentecost 15)*
              Neighbour   *(Pentecost 16)*

Unit 5   *Evidence of Faith*   *(Pentecost 17)*
              Quality of Faith   *(Pentecost 18)*
              Living Faith   *(Pentecost 19)*
              Enduring Faith   *(Pentecost 20)*

Unit 6   *Hoping*   *(Pentecost 21)*
              Choosing   *(Pentecost 22)*
              Waiting   *(Pentecost 23)*

Basic Preparation
As you begin *Seeds of the Word* for each unit, don't forget to recall pages 23–7. Agree **why, where** and **how** you are meeting; also decide on the allocation of **ministries**.

Pentecost 2, 3, 4 (Unit 1)

These three sessions are all based on John 15 and are about a community model of the Church.

> *Being the People of God*
> *Being Friends of God*
> *Being Free for God*

Preparing a focus for the Pentecost Season
(This focus can be used at any time during the season.)
Near my home in London is Hampton Court Palace. In one of the glasshouses is a vine which goes back to the time of Henry VIII. Every year it yields a harvest of grapes, and the vine-dresser is very proud of the quality of the crop. Vines, or vineyards, are planted when people feel safe enough to stay in one place. Ancient vineyards in places like Italy and Spain reflect the security of people and their long history.

Clusters of fresh grapes look beautiful. During the next three sessions why not create a bowl of grapes as a focus, sharing small clusters as you part each week, a reminder of your belonging together?

The Liturgical Colour is **green** and you might wish to cut greenery or place a plant on a small table as a further element to your focus. Be as creative as you can!

Use the following meditative prayer as you begin this unit:

> Powerfully
> I am drawn to that which has grown slowly
> and driven its roots deeply
> which has permanence and knows the pain of growth.

To grow is my wish
But am I prepared to receive the wounds of life?
To let any weather pass over me?
Am I ready to give shelter to many
Yet to seek shelter only with you?

I want to be radiant from the inside
I want to stand firm and to mature
To grow into you
To drive my roots deeply
To live through you
But I know
That the price is high.[1]

Pentecost 2

Getting started
As you look back over your life, what is the most meaningful
sense of community, or belonging to a group that you have
had? Why was it so special?

Read John 15:1–5.
(Other readings: Exodus 19:1–6; 1 Peter 2:1–10.)

1   **I am the true vine,**
    and my Father is the vinedresser.
2   **Every branch in me that bears no fruit**
    he cuts away,
    and every branch that does bear fruit he prunes
    to make it bear even more.
3   **You are clean already,**
    by means of the word that I have spoken to you.
    Remain in me, as I in you.
4   **As a branch cannot bear fruit all by itself,**
    unless it remains part of the vine,
    neither can you unless you remain in me.
5   **I am the vine,**

you are the branches.
Whoever remains in me, with me in him,
bears fruit in plenty;
for cut off from me you can do nothing.

Comment

The Christian community that St. John wrote to was under
threat. These Christians saw themselves as different from
others. They were quite critical of the more mainstream
Church, seeing themselves as more exclusive. John reminds
them that Jesus called them to be 'a loving community', regardless of their awareness of other people's suspicion and hatred.
Communities in danger often use a meal to disguise the whole
purpose of their meeting. Jesus teaches the community as it
shares a meal, an activity which would arouse less suspicion,
and symbolises both hospitality and solidarity. Jesus reminds
the community, 'I am the vine, you are the branches' (v. 5) and
tells them he is giving his encouragement and instructions to
stop them from 'falling away' (John 16:1) in the face of immi-
nent persecution (16:33).

Vineyards symbolise for nomadic people a place of settling
down. 'A healthy vine is a multifaceted source of joy, providing
fruit to eat, economic sustenance, and wine for celebration.'[2]
Jesus signals that, although he is 'the true vine . . . my Father
is the vinedresser' – or grower (v. 1). The prophets taught that,
without God, wild grapes would grow, thorns choke the vine,
and the vineyard would be destroyed (Isaiah 5:1–6). Israel is
described as the vine (Isaiah 27:2–5). But it did not bear good
fruit: 'God expected fair judgement, but found injustice,
uprightness, but found cries of distress' (Isaiah 5:7).

The new community needed to be different, rather than
exclusive, by acting justly and hearing cries of distress. Members needed to recognise that each needed the other in the
struggle. 'I am the true vine and my Father is the vinedresser . . .
make your home in me as I make mine in you' (vv. 1,4). Good
relationships within the community of disciples are the key to

the community's life and witness. Pietism, or calling themselves Christians, was not enough. The community must be seen to bear 'fruit in plenty' (v. 5).

Pruned trees bear heavier crops. Yet the image of pruning is an uncomfortable one, for branches get cut down and thrown away, and there is destruction in the process. We must remember that John wrote this for a community seeking to resist heavy pressure to conform to the religious political and social norms around it. People did betray the community and members suffered persecution as a result. The pruning process meant that some people were thrown out. 'Of course, this is a very dangerous course of action . . . It is not always easy to tell the fruit bearers from the others, or whether a branch that is fallow one season, might, if left alone, bloom the next.'[3] This is not comfortable stuff, but it is the message of John, and we must recognise that the pressures on communities under persecution are enormous. Being the people of God calls for ways of living that challenge the accepted norms, and seek to resist the pressure to conform.

Talking Points

> For those who think of the Christian Church as an all-inclusive body that welcomes and embraces people unconditionally, this is a jarring message. While all may be welcomed, only those who bear fruit are allowed to stay. In a situation of persecution, betrayal and suffering, there is no room for the purely contemplative or those who find simplistic salvation in calling oneself a Christian. It is not a place for bystanders, but for those whose connection to the vine brings life to others.[4]

How do you as a group respond to this statement? Is there a place for this kind of community in today's world? What are the dangers?

Reflection and Action

What kind of community of faith do you want? How inclusive
do you want it to be? Where are the signs of injustice and the
cries of distress around you? Does the community you envisage
want to do anything about the injustice and distress? What?
How?

Worship

Keep silence for a few moments. Then offer the following
prayer – ask two people to lead it:

READER 1:   Jesus said,
READER 2:   I am the true vine.
ALL: We are the branches.
READER 1:   Jesus said,
READER 2:   A branch cannot bear fruit all by itself
ALL: Unless it remains part of the vine.
READER 1:   Jesus said,
READER 2:   Whoever remains in me
ALL: Bears fruit in plenty.

Offer some short prayers for your community, group, for those
crying out for justice and in distress. After each prayer, say:

   Remain in me, as I in you.

Close with the Lord's Prayer.

Pentecost 3

Getting started

Review the week's world news. What has been the issue that
has made you think, 'There must be a better way to resolve
this problem'?

Read John 15:5–11.
(Other readings: Deuteronomy 6:17-end; Romans 6:3–11.)

5   I am the vine,
   you are the branches.
   Whoever remains in me, with me in him,
   bears fruit in plenty;
   for cut off from me you can do nothing.

6   Anyone who does not remain in me
   is thrown away like a branch
   – and withers;
   these branches are collected and thrown on the fire
   and are burnt.

7   If you remain in me
   and my words remain in you,
   you may ask for whatever you please
   and you will get it.

8   It is to the glory of my Father that you should bear much
   fruit and be my disciples.

9   I have loved you
   just as the Father has loved me.
   Remain in my love.

10 If you keep my commandments
   you will remain in my love,
   just as I have kept my Father's commandments
   and remain in his love.

11 I have told you this
   so that my own joy may be in you
   and your joy be complete.

Comment

'... Keep my commandments'. This is the insistent message
of Jesus, and we might feel like saying, 'Don't keep on ... we
get the point.' 'But alas, the problem is that we *do not* get the
message, for if people kept the commandment to love one
another, what a different world we would live in!'[5] So often
the Church is an embarrassment because Christian people are

not seen as people who love one another. John's community faced a hostile world, and the ever-present risk of persecution made disagreement dangerous. It was essential for their future wellbeing that they obey Jesus' command to love, thereby demonstrating solidarity to each other in the face of their enemies.

' "Love" would mean not only affection and a general kindliness, but standing with others in the community against betrayal, against outsiders and participating actively in creating the new communal bonds that must take the place of lost synagogue fellowship.'[6] The community acts in the light of a role model – 'I have loved you just as the Father has loved me,' says Jesus (v. 9).

Persecution came from the Romans to both Christians and Jews. As a result of interrogations, many Christians recanted. It was a criminal offence to make a public declaration for Jesus, claiming him as 'Sovereign Lord'. Such a title was in direct conflict with the Roman cult of emperor worship. John's Gospel was probably completed before 110 AD when Pliny, the emissary of the Emperor Trajan, devised a formula to test Christians who said they no longer believed: they were 'to curse the name of Christ and revere the image of Caesar.' Against this threat of compromise John's community was challenged by Jesus' teaching to 'remain in me' and 'keep my commandments' (vv. 9–10). For 'what counts above all in terms of the life of a Christian community is that its members have the courage to stand firm and give steady witness to their belief in Jesus.'[7]

Friendship with God is first expressed through solidarity with others who consider themselves friends of God. There is no room for compromise.

Talking Points

'One of the great ironies of Christian history,' writes Wes Howard-Brook, '[is that] the church has largely not been a model of what its own founder preached so many times that we get bored with hearing it.' What examples can you think of that bear out the truth of that statement? What individuals or

groups do you know of who have practised love that includes
'affection and a general kindliness', but have also stood with
others in the community against betrayal, whether by individuals or authorities? How can you as a group be more faithful
in keeping the commandment to love?

Reflection and Action

John's community was being prepared to stick together in the
realisation that difficult choices were going to face them. So
often when difficult ethical, moral or political situations face
Christians today they are unprepared to deal with them, and
either do nothing, or follow the prevailing trend. What are the
issues that you as a Christian group face? **Make a list.** Choose
one or two and decide how you will prepare yourselves to act,
and face any opposition that you might encounter.

Worship

Ask two people to read John 15:1–11. It is printed above line
by line; let reader one read the first line; reader two the second,
and so on. Look at the list of issues you as a group face, ask
someone to read them out one by one; after each is read,
everyone should say together:

> If you remain in me
> and my words remain in you,
> you may ask for whatever you please
> and you will get it.

Then read the two issues on which you have decided to take
action; all should say:

> Whoever remains in me, with me in him,
> bears fruit in plenty;
> for cut off from me you can do nothing . . .
> Remain in my love.

For next week prepare a simple meal. Let each person bring

a favourite dish. Ask some people to prepare prayers and readings on the theme *Love one another*.

Next week's Gospel is John 15:12–17.

Pentecost 4

Getting started

Who was your first real friend? Tell the group what was so special about them, and why you liked them. What was the most sacrificial thing they did for you, or you for them?

Read John 15:12–17.
(Other readings: Deuteronomy 7:6–11; Galatians 3:23–4:7.)

12 **This is my commandment:**
    love one another,
    as I have loved you.

13 **No one can have greater love**
    than to lay down his life for his friends.

14 **You are my friends,**
    if you do what I command you.

15 **I shall no longer call you servants,**
    because a servant does not know
    his master's business;
    I call you friends,
    because I have made known to you
    everything I learnt from my Father.

16 **You did not choose me,**
    no, I chose you;
    and I commissioned you
    to go out and to bear fruit,
    fruit that will last;
    so that the Father will give you
    anything you ask him in my name.

17 **My command to you**
    is to love one another.

Comment

'The laying down of life is not an abstract model of general
self-sacrifice, but an expression of commitment that flows
directly from the relationship among "friends." '8 The Gospel
of John recalls John the Baptist 'laying down his life' for Jesus
by saying, 'his influence must increase, and mine decrease.'
John the Baptist died a martyr's death (Mark 6:17–29), and he
provided an all-too-poignant example of the 'greater love'
which lays down life. Jesus' decision, and invitation to follow
the same path, is crystal clear, and there is a cost to be counted
(Mark 8:34–6).

If the disciples follow, they will no longer be slaves or servants. The act of following shows they have understood God's
purpose for them; now they will be 'in the know' of God's plan.
So by choosing to 'lay down life' as well as 'keep the commandment to love one another', they find themselves chosen to fulfil
God's mission (v. 16). The mission task is to 'bear fruit that
will last' (v. 16). In a society that was governed by hours of
daylight journeys at walking pace, and tightly ordered and
status-conscious communities, 'bearing fruit' needed to be practical. The apostles (Acts 2:43–7; 4:32; 5:12ff.) taught that fruit
was seen in terms of 'mutual care, especially in having financial
concern for the poor. Sharing common meals and solidarity
with other Christian communities was also important. Bearing
fruit also meant respect, tenderness, fulfilling one's domestic
duties, joy, patience, sharing one's goods with the needy'
(Romans 12:9–13).9

The most controversial area of 'bearing fruit' in a class-
ridden society lay in the 'abolition of distinctions of roles and
status'.10 Baptism into the Christian faith meant 'there can be
neither Jew nor Greek, there can be neither slave nor free
man, there can be neither male nor female – for you are all one
in Christ Jesus' (Galatians 3:28). Fruit-bearing is a continuous
process: day by day, people need to go on practising togetherness, showing love, equality, humility and concern for one
another, especially the poor. God's mission is the continuous

practice of 'the best way of all' (1 Corinthians 12:31) consistently lived out in the ordinariness of everyday life.

Talking Points
'Bearing fruit that will last' is essentially an everyday commitment to simple virtues lived in obedience to the command of Jesus to 'love one another'. Why is it that we find it so difficult to be consistent? What individuals or groups of people do we discriminate against? Why? How do we make effective in our lives as individuals and a group that 'all are one in Christ Jesus'?

Reflection, Action and Worship
How are you as a group 'sticking together' in facing the issues you have chosen to act on? What out of today's **Comment** and **Talking Points** has helped you for the next stage of your journey together?

Pray for each other – thanking God for your experience of community. Conclude by saying aloud the names of the people who were your first real friends, and praying together: 'Lord, remember them in love.'

What will you do now? Unit 2 covering Pentecost 5–10 is a six-session programme exploring:

New Law
New Humanity
New Way
New Fruit
New Resources
New Mind

Pentecost 5

Getting started
Have you ever had to trust someone you did not know with something or someone important to you?

Read Matthew 19:16–26.
(Other readings: Exodus 20:1–17; Ephesians 5:1–10.)

16 A man came to him and asked, 'Master, what good deed
17 must I do to possess eternal life?' Jesus said to him, 'Why do
you ask me about what is good? There is one alone who is
good. But if you wish to enter into life, keep the command-
18 ments.' He said, 'Which ones?' Jesus replied, 'These: You
shall not kill. You shall not commit adultery. You shall not
19 steal. You shall not give false witness. Honour your father
and your mother. You shall love your neighbour as yourself.'
20 The young man said to him, 'I have kept all these. What more
21 do I need to do?' Jesus said, 'If you wish to be perfect, go
and sell your possessions and give the money to the poor, and
22 you will have treasure in heaven; then come, follow me.' But
when the young man heard these words he went away sad,
for he was a man of great wealth.
23   Then Jesus said to his disciples, 'In truth I tell you, it is
24 hard for someone rich to enter the kingdom of Heaven. Yes,
I tell you again, it is easier for a camel to pass through the
eye of a needle than for someone rich to enter the kingdom of
25 Heaven.' When the disciples heard this they were astonished.
26 'Who can be saved then?' they said. Jesus gazed at them. 'By
human resources', he told them, 'this is impossible; for God
everything is possible.'

Comment

A rich man wanted to receive religious salvation and asked,
'What good deed must I do to possess eternal life?' (v. 16)
Jesus told him what good deed to do: 'go and sell your possessions and give the money to the poor, and through that
action you will have eternal life, "treasure in heaven".' The
wealthy man did not want salvation on such terms. Salvation
in this form also raised questions among Jesus' closest followers: 'Who can be saved, then?' (v. 25)

   This story was a powerful criticism of wealth, and the way
in which wealth was accumulated. The man who came to Jesus

had 'great wealth' (v. 22) and it was measured in land, farms, fields and estates. Despite protests that he had kept the commandments, Jesus exposed the rich man's failure in neighbourly love. By calling him to sell his possessions and give to the poor, Jesus was seeking both redistribution and reparation. Land was frequently acquired as payment for loans, particularly in times of bad harvest. Far from being blameless, Jesus revealed the landowner as someone who had become wealthy by defrauding the poor.

Writing for increasingly prosperous Christian communities, Matthew's Gospel declares that the most potent sign of God's reign lies in people 'doing good'. 'If persons, especially those whose possessions guaranteed them status and wealth, would love their neighbours as themselves, individual needs would be balanced with wider communal needs. Meeting communal needs would be the sign of proper self-love. The kingdom of God is simply that time, that place in which *there are no rich and poor*.'[11]

To receive the Kingdom of God is to experience a changed attitude towards power and wealth. For the rich, repentance is to be an act of reparation to the poor for what has been taken from them. Jewish law required the remission of all debts every fifty years – a Jubilee (Leviticus 25.) The law was flouted, but Jesus revived the Jubilee principle in the story of the rich man, showing that this was part of salvation. Putting Jubilee into practice meant a dramatic social change – a reversal of traditional power structures. By choosing to retain control over his property, the rich man not only denied himself access to the Kingdom, but continued the cycle of oppression and poverty which his inherited wealth had caused.

Talking Points
'We simply cannot get around Jesus' discipleship instructions to the rich: we lack only one thing – to follow we must *give back*.'[12] Do you agree?

Christian people prefer to interpret this story in a way that

says if you are rich you must not let your wealth get in the
way of your love for God and the Church. But that is to reject
the thrust of the story. Redistributing wealth in our world is
not a popular idea, any more than it was for the rich man, but
the gospel seems to demand it, and sees it as one of the ways
in which the Kingdom of God comes on 'earth as it is in
heaven.' What are the implications of 'go, sell your surplus
possessions and give to the poor' for ourselves, the Church,
and the community of nations?

Reflection and Action

There are only two reasons why human beings actively
challenge the way things are in the world. One is that they
are deviant or crazy. The other reason is that they have
convictions regarding alternative possibilities for individual and collective living. For Jesus, a conviction about
an alternative reality he called the kingdom of God (Mark
1:15) drove his struggle to change the way things are, and
underpinned his invitation to radical discipleship.[13]

Do you agree?

One of the purposes of *Seeds of the Word* is to encourage
the formation of small intentional communities that will act as
a sort of counterculture. Simply, we need each other to live out
the values of the gospel, and this story more than any other
reveals that need for solidarity as we seek to live out Jesus'
commands.

What 'alternative possibilities for individual and collective
living' can you as a group envisage? Are there small steps you
can take together now towards such possibilities?

Worship

LEADER: Lord, you call us to 'build a new world in the shell
of the old.'[14]

ALL: We lack only one thing – to follow we must give
back.

LEADER:	If you wish to enter life,
ALL:	Keep the commandments.
LEADER:	You shall love your neighbour as yourself.
ALL:	Who then can be saved?
LEADER:	By human resources, this is impossible;
ALL:	For God everything is possible.

Worship co-ordinators should produce copies of the hymn 'Thou who was rich beyond all splendour'.[15] Keep a moment of silence, and then either read the hymn aloud, or sing it together.

Pentecost 6

Getting started

Have you ever made friends with someone whom other people rejected, or disliked? What happened?

Read Luke 15: 11–end.
(Other readings: Exodus 24:3–11; Colossians 3:12–17.)

11,12 Then Jesus said, 'There was a man who had two sons. ● The younger one said to his father, "Father, let me have the share of the estate that will come to me." So the father

13 divided the property between them. A few days later, the younger son got together everything he had and left for a distant country where he squandered his money on a life of debauchery.

14 'When he had spent it all, that country experienced a
15 severe famine, and now he began to feel the pinch; so he hired himself out to one of the local inhabitants who put
16 him on his farm to feed the pigs. And he would willingly have filled himself with the husks the pigs were eating, but
17 no one would let him have them. Then he came to his senses and said, "How many of my father's hired men have
18 all the food they want and more, and here am I dying of hunger! I will leave this place and go to my father and say:

19 Father, I have sinned against heaven and against you; I no
20 longer deserve to be called your son; treat me as one of
    your hired men." So he left the place and went back to his
    father.

    'While he was still a long way off, his father saw him and
    was moved with pity. He ran to the boy, clasped him in his
21 arms and kissed him. Then his son said, "Father, I have
    sinned against heaven and against you. I no longer deserve
22 to be called your son." But the father said to his servants,
    "Quick! Bring out the best robe and put it on him; put a
23 ring on his finger and sandals on his feet. Bring the calf we
    have been fattening, and kill it: we will celebrate by having
24 a feast, because this son of mine was dead and has come
    back to life; he was lost and is found." And they began to
    celebrate.

25 'Now the elder son was out in the fields, and on his way
    back, as he drew near the house, he could hear music and
26 dancing. Calling one of the servants he asked what it was
27 all about. The servant told him, "Your brother has come,
    and your father has killed the calf we had been fattening
28 because he has got him back safe and sound." He was
    angry then and refused to go in, and his father came out
29 and began to urge him to come in; but he retorted to his
    father, "All these years I have slaved for you and never
    once disobeyed any orders of yours, yet you never offered
30 me so much as a kid for me to celebrate with my friends.
    But, for this son of yours, when he comes back after swal-
    lowing up your property – he and his loose women – you
    kill the calf we had been fattening."

31 'The father said, "My son, you are with me always and
32 all I have is yours. But it was only right that we should
    celebrate and rejoice, because your brother here was dead
    and has come to life; he was lost and is found." '

Comment

'Dad, I wish you were dead!' That is the shocking implication of the request of the young son to his healthy father, as he asked for his share of the inheritance. It would not have been unreasonable for a father to get angry and disinherit his son, but this is not what happened. This is a story with a difference. The inheritance was shared (v. 12), the prodigal quickly turned his portion into cash, a task that normally took months in Middle Eastern society. Then he went 'to a far country'. And the rest, as they say, 'is history'.

The prodigal left behind him the legacy of a humiliated father, an un-reconciled brother, and a hostile, tightly-knit community. After his 'life of debauchery' (v. 13) and the discomfort of a severe famine, the young man found himself without resources or friends. He got work with ceremonially unclean animals, a gesture tantamount to a brush-off. Hunger forced him to consider that he would be better off being a hired man back home.

> A hired man was a free man with his own income, living independently in the local village. His social status would not be inferior to that of his father and his brother. He could keep his pride and maintain his independence. But there was more: if the prodigal became a hired servant, he might be able to pay back what he had lost.[16]

In exile, such reasoning sounded well; in the village, the reality would be different. The father knew this, and while perhaps he expected the boy to fail, his actions were totally out of character for a Middle Eastern landowner. Knowing the boy would be mocked, taunted, even physically attacked if he returned, the father watched out for him and saw him when 'he was still a long way off'. 'Moved with pity' (v. 20), the father sought to prevent his son running the gauntlet of gathering villagers. Out of keeping with the dignity of a man of status, 'he ran to the boy, clasped him in his arms' (v. 21) – kissing him again and again. The wide-eyed villagers, taking their cue from the father,

would accept the young man back. Such generosity of spirit
was outside of their experience; no wronged father would act
like this – and there are no other stories in Middle Eastern
literature that are like this one. By giving him the 'best robe'
to wear, probably his own, the father ensures the son's rehabili-
tation in the community; the ring indicates trust, and the shoes
that he is 'a free man in the house, not a servant.'

Angry at the father's generosity, the older son now humili-
ates him by quarrelling in front of the guests (vv. 28–9). Accu-
sations of favouritism fly (vv. 29–30), and the older son's idea
of joy, 'a kid for me to celebrate with my friends' (v. 30),
reveals his failure to understand the joy that comes from resto-
ration and forgiveness.

Jesus tells this story, and two others in Luke 15, in the
company of scribes and Pharisees, religious lawyers critical of
his association with the outcasts of society. The parable speaks
of two rebels, one within the system, and the other outside it.
The message to the listening Pharisees is clear: do what the
father did – accept repentance, be reconciled and choose joy.
This is the pattern for the New Humanity.

Talking Points

All the elements of the Christian gospel are present in this
story. Spend a few moments discussing together where you see
sin, repentance, grace, joy and sonship in this parable. What is
the impact and effect of each?

Reflection, Action and Worship

Have someone read aloud Colossians 3:12–17 – this is one of
the *Other Readings* for Pentecost 6. These are guidelines for
people living in community. Discuss together how you will
make this passage a basis for dealing with each other as you
become a group together.

For a few moments let each person reflect in silence and
then, without comment, say out loud the grace they most need
to 'put on'. For example, one might say, 'kindness'; another,

'compassion'. It doesn't matter if someone has already chosen the grace you need. When each person has made clear the grace they most need, say together:

> As God's chosen ones we put on the graces of compassion, kindness, lowliness, meekness and patience.

Reflect now on those situations in which you both need to forgive and to be forgiven. Keep a few moments' silence and then say:

> Help us, Lord, to bear with one another,
> and not hold on to resentment.
> Help us to forgive and receive forgiveness.
> Give us grace to put on the gift of love,
> make us thankful,
> and may the peace of Christ reign in our hearts.

For next week: Look in the newspapers and other media and note stories where people seem to find it impossible to forgive.

Pentecost 7

Getting started

What examples have you discovered where people have found it impossible to forgive? Discuss together for a while, then ask each person to repeat their example one at a time, and in between each make the response: 'Lord, how often must I forgive when I am wronged?' When you have finished, ask two people to read today's Scripture passage, one reading Peter's questions and responses; and the other reading those of Jesus. Say together the Lord's Prayer, stopping at the phrase: 'Forgive us our sins as we forgive those who have sinned against us.'

Read Matthew 18:21-end.
(Other readings: Hosea 11:1–9; 1 Corinthians 12:27–13:end.)

21 Peter went up to Jesus and said, 'Lord, how often must I forgive my brother if he wrongs me? As often as seven times?'

22 Jesus answered, 'Not seven, I tell you, but seventy-seven times.

23 'And so the kingdom of Heaven may be compared to a king who decided to settle his accounts with his servants.
24 When the reckoning began, they brought him a man who
25 owed ten thousand talents; he had no means of paying, so his master gave orders that he should be sold, together with his wife and children and all his possessions, to meet the debt.
26 At this the servant threw himself down at his master's feet with the words, "Be patient with me and I will pay the whole
27 sum." And the servant's master felt so sorry for him that he
28 let him go and cancelled the debt. Now as this servant went out, he happened to meet a fellow-servant who owed him one hundred denarii, and he seized him by the throat, and
29 began to throttle him, saying, "Pay what you owe me." His fellow-servant fell at his feet and appealed to him, saying,
30 "Be patient with me and I will pay you." But the other would not agree; on the contrary, he had him thrown into prison
31 till he should pay the debt. His fellow-servants were deeply distressed when they saw what had happened and they went
32 to their master and reported the whole affair to him. Then the master sent for the man and said to him, "You wicked servant, I cancelled all that debt of yours when you appealed
33 to me. Were you not bound, then, to have pity on your fellow-
34 servant just as I had pity on you?" And in his anger the master handed him over to the torturers until he should pay
35 all his debt. And that is how my heavenly Father will deal with you unless you each forgive your brother from your heart.'

Comment

'I can never forgive', screamed the headline of a local news-paper quoting a war veteran tortured and imprisoned in Asia during the Second World War. In four short words, he summar-ises the most difficult task faced by the human community – forgiveness. Matthew is writing to a group of churches divided

by problems in relationships, ethnic differences, and the failure
to share resources so that there were not some who 'have' and
others who 'have not'. Matthew 18 is about dealing with the
roots of the problems that cause division by asking, 'Who is
the greatest?' (vv. 1–4) It reveals carelessness for the 'little
ones' (v. 10), those who are socially and economically powerless; and a lack of awareness for those outside the fold (vv.
12–14).

If the Christian community is to be different, so that it can
be 'salt' and 'light' (Matthew 5:13–16) it must be a visible
alternative. Christians should exercise humility, giving up rank
and status, to 'become like little children' (v. 3). In practice
this means seeking out those alienated by pride, power and
wealth (vv. 10–14), correcting one another, and being reconciled (vv. 15–18), so that prayer can be offered to achieve
real and lasting change (vv. 18–20).

Forgiving brothers and sisters from the heart (v. 35) is a
notoriously difficult task. Broken relationships are bad enough,
but when material debt is involved too, then in most communities it is another matter altogether. Jesus demonstrates how
difficult handling other people's debt is in this demanding and
unnerving parable (vv. 18–35). Matthew required his churches
to practise mercy (5:7). In both Greek and Aramaic 'mercy'
means 'an integrated or holistic state of mind characterised by
understanding, compassion and justice. Merciful people act out
of their own integrity by being open to the needs around
them.'[17] It is this quality of integrity that Matthew calls the
Christian community to embrace and practise in their
relationships.

Matthew 18 is written as a corrective, reminding people of
what they already know, but have neglected or forgotten. Jesus'
concern for the 'little ones' extends to concern for their
material well-being. If poorer members of the community were
suffering under the burden of debt, usually brought about
through money owed to landowners in times of poor harvest,
and richer members of the community failed to help remit that

debt, the Christian community was failing to live up to Jesus' vision for God's new order. Unity and peace in the church, let alone the world, cannot happen until forgiveness is practised both in relationships and in practical material ways too. In the Lord's Prayer, the original reads, 'forgive us our debts – as we forgive those indebted to us' (6:12). The practice of Jubilee (see *Pentecost 6 – Comment*) is to be the day-by-day practice of the Christian community. No wonder 'the common people heard Jesus gladly' (Mark 12:37). Such behaviour consistently lived out would be a *New Way* indeed.

Talking Points

'In the "Our Father," then, Jesus is not simply recommending vaguely that we might pardon those who have bothered us or made us trouble, but tells us purely and simply to erase the debts of those who owe us money; which is to say, practice the jubilee.'[18] What are the implications of this kind of debt forgiveness? Do you have any examples or experience of this kind of forgiveness happening at a personal level? Is this the kind of behaviour that the Church should be encouraging? How?

A professor at Princeton University in the USA, Alan Blinder, talking about the debt owed by many developing countries, has said: 'The rich countries may soon have to choose between partial forgiveness and unilateral repudiation. Forgiveness is the better alternative.' Do you agree?

Reflection and Action

Are there situations where forgiveness of debt, either in relationships or materially, is necessary in your church or community, or where perhaps you should take steps personally? What action can you take both as an individual, and as a group? Find out what bodies like the *Debt Crisis Network* and *Jubilee 2000*[19] are attempting to do to have international debt remitted, and see how you can help.

Worship
Say together this version of the Lord's Prayer:

> Our Father in heaven,
> hallowed be your name,
> your kingdom come, on earth as in heaven.
> Give us today our daily bread,
> (*pause*) and give daily bread to . . . (*offer suggestions for
>   those deprived of daily food*).
> Forgive our debts,
> as we forgive those in debt to us . . . as individuals, as
>   nations (*offer suggestions of nations who are in debt*).
> Do not bring us to the time of trial.
> (*pause, offer short prayers for those facing trials of
>   different kinds*).
> Deliver us, and all people, from evil,
> for the kingdom, the power and the glory are yours
> for ever, and for ever. Amen.

For next week, plan a simple meal together. Begin with a
short liturgy, which the worship co-ordinator should ask someone to prepare on the theme *For God everything is possible*.

Select some situations in which it seems impossible for forgiveness to be offered, and as each situation is mentioned,
make the response: 'In human terms this is impossible; for God
everything is possible.' Discuss over your meal how you as a
group are growing together.

Pentecost 8

Getting started
Begin with worship on the theme *For God everything is
possible*.

Read John 15:6–end.
(Other readings: Ezekiel 36:24–8; Galatians 5:16–25.)

16 You did not choose me,
  no, I chose you;
  and I commissioned you
  to go out and to bear fruit,
  fruit that will last;
  so that the Father will give you
  anything you ask him in my name.

17 My command to you
  is to love one another.

18 If the world hates you,
  you must realise that it hated me before it hated you.

19 If you belonged to the world,
  the world would love you as its own;
  but because you do not belong to the world,
  because my choice of you has drawn you out of the world,
  that is why the world hates you.

20 Remember the words I said to you:
  A servant is not greater than his master.
  If they persecuted me,
  they will persecute you too;
  if they kept my word,
  they will keep yours as well.

21 But it will be on my account that they will do all this to you,
  because they do not know the one who sent me.

22 If I had not come,
  if I had not spoken to them,
  they would have been blameless;
  but as it is they have no excuse for their sin.

23 Anyone who hates me hates my Father.

24 If I had not performed such works among them
  as no one else has ever done,
  they would be blameless;
  but as it is, in spite of what they have seen,
  they hate both me and my Father.

25   But all this was only to fulfil the words written in their Law:
     They hated me without reason.
26   When the Paraclete comes,
     whom I shall send to you from the Father,
     the Spirit of truth who issues from the Father,
     he will be my witness.
27   And you too will be witnesses,
     because you have been with me from the beginning.

Comment

'I hate you' is a phrase we associate with children in the play-
ground, rather than an emotion expressed by mature adults.
Yet hate is an all-too-present reality in our contemporary
world, evidenced by civil wars, racial and internecine violence,
and in countless family feuds. The Old Testament is realistic
about hate. Esau plotted to kill Jacob (Genesis 27:41), and
Joseph's brothers had him exiled because of their jealousy
(Genesis 37:5–8).

The Psalms are full of hate! To sensitive and sophisticated
Westerners, the opposition expressed towards those who do not
love God is difficult to take. Sometimes even God is revealed as
one who hates, albeit injustice and violence (Psalm 31:6). So
when Jesus talked about the destiny of the Christian community to be 'hated', it was hardly a new idea. Jesus warned
the community that, like him, they will experience hatred and
rejection. He advises the Christian community that those who
are part of the system ('the world', v. 18) know how to gain
the support of others in the system. 'But,' says Jesus, 'because
you are not part of the system, but have been chosen by me
to be out of the system, the system will hate you.'

In practical terms, the kind of challenge that faces the Church
has been expressed like this: 'The consequences for our modern
church relationships with governments and culturally acceptable practices are all too clear: each time we stand as Christians
in support of the violence of war, racism, or nationalism, we
betray the call to which Jesus has chosen to answer.'[20]

There is a cost to contemporary discipleship, if people are prepared to face it: this is the challenge of John. At the same time only a masochist or someone with a martyr complex would enjoy the prospect of suffering for the Christian or any cause. Most people face persecution with great trepidation. To respond to the call, people need both the inspiration and the assurance of the solidarity and comfort of the Spirit of God in their suffering.

In the light of the dangers involved in responding to the challenge of Christian discipleship, the earlier insistence by Jesus that people should 'love one another' exposes also the real possibility of 'laying down their lives for their friends' (v. 13).

Talking Points
In what ways have you seen the 'system' at work in your locality, work-place, country? Where do you see hatred being expressed? Do you agree that 'each time we stand as Christians in support of the violence of war, racism, or nationalism, we betray the call which Jesus has chosen to answer'?

Reflection and Action
No one in their right mind chooses to suffer for any cause. To take a stand for what is right can lead to criticism, scorn, and for many people around the world torture, imprisonment and death. Are there people you know of who are suffering for the sake of justice? How can you act in solidarity and offer comfort in the Spirit of God?

Sometimes 'people suffer for the sake of justice' actually means 'suffer for the *lack* of justice'. Do you know such people? How can you help them in their struggle for a more just and equal share of things?

Worship
For the next time, use the Liturgy for Justice on page 241. You may want to adapt it for your situation, so plan carefully.

Pentecost 9

Getting started
Begin with the Liturgy for Justice on page 241.

Read Ephesians 6:10–20.
(Other readings: Joshua 1:1–9; John 17:11–19.)

10 Finally, grow strong in the Lord, with the strength of his
11 power. Put on the full armour of God so as to be able to
12 resist the devil's tactics. For it is not against human enemies
     that we have to struggle, but against the principalities and
     the ruling forces who are masters of the darkness in this
13 world, the spirits of evil in the heavens. That is why you must
     take up all God's armour, or you will not be able to put up
     any resistance on the evil day, or stand your ground even
     though you exert yourselves to the full.

14 So stand your ground, with truth a belt round your waist,
15 and uprightness a breastplate, wearing for shoes on your feet
16 the eagerness to spread the gospel of peace and always carry-
     ing the shield of faith so that you can use it to quench the
17 burning arrows of the Evil One. And then you must take
     salvation as your helmet and the sword of the Spirit, that is,
     the word of God.

18 In all your prayer and entreaty keep praying in the Spirit
     on every possible occasion. Never get tired of staying awake
19 to pray for all God's holy people, and pray for me to be given
     an opportunity to open my mouth and fearlessly make known
20 the mystery of the gospel of which I am an ambassador in
     chains; pray that in proclaiming it I may speak as fearlessly
     as I ought to.

Comment

'One of the most pressing questions facing the world today is,
"How can we oppose evil without creating new evils and being
made evil ourselves?" '[21] Christian people are called, not to
destroy people, but to change the systems which dehumanise,

enslave, disempower and destroy the humanity of others. To do this work requires the use of spiritual weapons, 'the full armour of God' (6:10), including justice, peace, faith, salvation, the Word of God and prayer. The writer of Ephesians puts the challenge in terms of a conflict: 'against the principalities and the ruling forces who are masters of darkness in this world, the spirits of evil in the heavens' (v. 12).

These 'principalities and ruling forces' or 'Powers' are the systems and structures which dominate our world, 'and they are not simply evil. They can be not only benign but quite positive', says Walter Wink in his remarkable trilogy.[22] 'It is precisely because the Powers have been created in, through, and for the humanizing purposes of God in Christ that they must be honoured, criticised, resisted and redeemed.'

Simply put:

> The Powers are good.
> The Powers are fallen.
> The Powers must be redeemed.

The fallen nature of the Powers is witnessed in abuse of power by governments, organisations, multinational companies, but also in racism, sexism, political and economic oppression, violence, militarism, ecological destruction, greed, patriarchy, and homelessness – to name but a few!

To struggle against the Powers that threaten our humanity is the calling of all God's people. No one is exempt from complicity in the way the system dehumanises. But as Wink argues, 'the church's peculiar calling is to discern and engage both the structure and the spirituality of oppressive institutions.' The Christian task is to pray, to take a stand, seeking to discern the true nature of things, allowing truth to hold things together like 'a belt around your waist' (v. 14). If our prayer is informed by the desire for justice, then our own lives should wear 'uprightness [justice] as a breastplate' (v. 14). For the purpose of transforming the way things are is 'to spread the gospel of peace' (v. 15). Peace here is seen as 'wholeness' or 'harmony'. Those who pray, seek a desirable future, one in which everyone will 'have an opportunity to open [their] mouth' and speak 'fearlessly' (v. 19).

Talking Points

Prayer is not about sending a letter to some sort of celestial Santa's grotto. It is more an act of co-creation and co-working with God. It is about believing a different future into being. 'It is,' as Wink says, 'far from being an escape from action, a means of focusing for action and of creating action.' Does this way of praying make sense to you? What opportunities does this way of praying open up for you?

Prayer is not us reminding God what ought to be done, but rather God reminding us what he is doing and seeking our collaboration. 'When we turn to pray,' says Wink, 'it is already the second step of prayer. We join with God in a prayer already going on in us and in the world.' What should this say to us about the place of silence, listening and discerning what tasks we should pick up and what ones to leave for others?

Reflection and Action

If our prayer is informed by the desire for justice, then our lives should wear 'uprightness [justice] as a breastplate'. How can you as individuals and as a group monitor 'uprightness' or justice in your own lives?

How can you work and pray in order to seek a desirable future, one in which everyone will 'have an opportunity to open their mouth' and speak 'fearlessly'?

Worship

In preparation for next time, the **worship co-ordinator** should read the following, and decide with others what to do.

Read the Gospel for PENTECOST 10, John 13:1–15, and incorporate it into the worship.

Next week marks the end of this unit of *Seeds of the Word*. Decide on some appropriate act or ritual to mark your life together and your struggle for justice. You may consider 'foot washing' to be appropriate, but think carefully before deciding. It may be possible for the group to share a simple Eucharist.

Organise an act of confession on the theme of the betrayal of justice.

Prepare intercessions on the theme of *Solidarity* with others. Conclude with the prayer:

> God, help me to refuse ever to accept evil; by your Spirit empower me to work for change precisely where and how you call me; and free me from thinking I have to do everything. (Walter Wink)

The next unit of *Seeds of the Word*:

Pentecost 11 *The Serving Community*
Pentecost 12 *The Witnessing Community*
Pentecost 13 *The Suffering Community*

Decide what you as a group are going to do. Will you continue to meet? When? Where?

Pentecost 10

Getting started
What is the greatest kindness anyone has shown to you? Share it with the group.

Read John 13:1–15.
(Other readings: Job 42:1–6, Philippians 2:1–11.)

1 Before the festival of the Passover, Jesus, knowing that his hour had come to pass from this world to the Father, having loved those who were his in the world, loved them to the end.

2 They were at supper, and the devil had already put it into
3 the mind of Judas Iscariot, son of Simon, to betray him. Jesus knew that the Father had put everything into his hands, and
4 that he had come from God and was returning to God, and he

got up from table, removed his outer garments and, taking a
5   towel, wrapped it round his waist; he then poured water into
a basin and began to wash the disciples' feet and to wipe
them with the towel he was wearing.
6   He came to Simon Peter who said to him, 'Lord, are you
7   going to wash my feet?' Jesus answered, 'At the moment
you do not know what I am doing, but later you will under-
8   stand.' 'Never!' said Peter. 'You shall never wash my feet.'
Jesus replied, 'If I do not wash you, you can have no share
9   with me.' Simon Peter said, 'Well then, Lord, not only my
10   feet, but my hands and my head as well!' Jesus said, 'No one
who has had a bath needs washing, such a person is clean all
11   over. You too are clean, though not all of you are.' He knew
who was going to betray him, and that was why he said,
'though not all of you are'.
12   When he had washed their feet and put on his outer garments again he went back to the table. 'Do you understand',
13   he said, 'what I have done to you? You call me Master and
14   Lord, and rightly; so I am. If I, then, the Lord and Master,
15   have washed your feet, you must wash each other's feet.
I have given you an example so that you may copy what I
have done to you.'

Comment

In many cultures feet are hidden, if only by sandals, and washing someone else's feet is a very intimate action. Probing the
spaces, feeling the callousness, observing the broken nails, is a
deeply personal experience for anyone of whatever class or
culture. 'To allow someone to wash our feet is to open ourselves
to an intimacy beyond the scope of most relationships.'[23] Perhaps we should not be surprised that Peter resisted something
so intimate. Although an intimate encounter, foot-washing was
undertaken by slaves in the society of Jesus' time. Peter clearly
felt that it was demeaning for Jesus to act in this way – and his
outspokenness possibly reflected the outlook of the rest of the
discipleship community.

Jesus washes feet 'knowing that his hour had come to pass from this world to the Father' (v. 1) – for 'he had come from God and was returning to God' (v. 3). John confidently reminds his readers where Jesus is from and what his destiny is. Jesus' sense of destiny is reflected in the term 'hour', which means a 'significant moment in time'. At this 'hour' betrayal, humiliation and execution are the immediate realities. For the moment the devil, like a strong man, has forced entry into the discipleship community, and Judas becomes the betrayer. Jesus, the Stronger Man (Mark 3:27), has known all along the inevitability of such action, and has warned of it (Mark 8:31). Far from seeing himself as a victim of the devil, Jesus has all along weighed up the consequences of his words and actions, calculating his time, and completing his mission. He has never been in any doubt that his chosen path would lead inevitably to martyrdom.

It is against this background that Jesus washes the feet of his disciples. He 'got up' – the word used here by John means 'resurrection' – and 'removed [laid aside] his outer garments' (v. 4). The imagery here is used by Jesus describing himself as 'the good shepherd who lays down his life for his sheep' (John 10:11, 15, 17, 18). As Wes Howard-Brook has commented, 'As Jesus will lay down his life freely, so he lays down his cloak, symbolic of his body.' By taking the towel and girding himself, Jesus invited the disciples to accept the reality of his coming death and to 'gird' (John 21:7, 18) themselves in preparation for their own death.

The disciples have their feet washed 'as an example' (v. 15), not of humility, but of preparing one another to face the possibility of death because of their discipleship to Jesus. As Jesus (the 'Master' vv. 13, 14, 16) could not avoid death, neither can the disciples (the 'servant' v. 16). People of faith who experience persecution because they proclaim God's truth in word and deed know the need for symbolic actions of support and comfort from each other, as well as outsiders. Such actions transform relationships and faith, to empower people to face whatever comes.

Talking Points, Reflection, Action and Worship
Sharing together with other people in discussion about things that matter to us, is an intimate and vulnerable act. What has been good for you as a group during these past few weeks? Give an example of something that someone else has said or done that has helped you in some way.

Offer the worship you have planned.

Before you leave the meeting, decide on your next encounter with *Seeds of the Word*.

Pentecost 11

Getting started
Share an occasion when you have felt let down or betrayed by someone.

Read John 13:31–5.
(Other readings: Isaiah 42:1–7; 2 Corinthians 4:1–10.)

31 **When he had gone, Jesus said:**
    Now has the Son of man been glorified,
    and in him God has been glorified.
32 **If God has been glorified in him,**
    God will in turn glorify him in himself,
    and will glorify him very soon.
33 **Little children,**
    I shall be with you only a little longer.
    You will look for me,
    and, as I told the Jews,
    where I am going
    you cannot come.
34 **I give you a new commandment:**
    love one another;
    you must love one another

just as I have loved you.

35   It is by your love for one another,
that everyone will recognise you
as my disciples.

Comment

'It was night' (v. 30). Judas Iscariot, having 'taken a piece of bread', symbolically sharing in the festival supper, 'went out' (v. 30). In these few words there is tension and drama. Within the close discipleship community a traitor had been exposed. Shortly before Judas's departure, Jesus had washed the feet of his disciples, in a gesture which he encouraged them to do for each other as an indication of support and encouragement in the face of persecution and possible death. When the traitor 'had gone' (v. 31), Jesus re-emphasised how important the lesson of 'loving one another' (v. 34) was in creating and maintaining a community able to resist betrayal, persecution and death. The very act of love of each other would be the means by which 'everyone will recognise you as my disciples' (v. 35).

This re-emphasis on the necessity to support and encourage each other by symbolic gestures, such as foot-washing, and by making their love for one another something to be observed, may have been difficult for the disciples to hear. After all, they had experienced betrayal by one of their own, Judas; and Jesus warned them again, 'I shall be with you only a little longer' and that where he was going 'you cannot come' (v. 33). Jesus had sought to console his disciples, but he could not protect them from the starkness of the realities that now faced both him and them. In coded language he spoke of the resurrection: 'where I am going you cannot come', and later, 'I am going now to prepare a place for you' (14:1).

Destructive forces are closing in on Jesus. His discipleship community is fragile, still full of misunderstanding (vv. 6–10), insecure because of betrayal (vv. 21–30), and confused about what it means to practise 'love for one another' when they really do not 'know' each other, and therefore trust each other.

Jesus, in giving his 'new commandment', also offers himself as an example of the process of loving even those you don't know or dare not trust. By commanding them 'to love one another just as I have loved you' (v. 34), Jesus says, in effect, 'I have put up with your failure to "know" me, your betrayals, distorted ambitions, criticism, inability to comprehend the real nature of my calling by God, and I have been consistent in my love of you. Now you do the same.'

Talking Points

How can we love people who we are not sure can be trusted? In practice, what does it mean to love those among us that we don't really know?

'It is by your love for one another that everyone will recognise you as my disciples.' Wes Howard-Brook comments, 'For all the missionary efforts of two thousand years of Christianity, whether the violence of the Crusades and conquistadors or the hard sell of today's television preachers and Bible beaters, no "strategy" would be as successful in bringing people within Jesus' sheepfold as the concrete witness of communities of mutual love.'[24] Why is it so difficult to form such communities?

Reflection and Action

When have you been touched by someone's kindness or generosity? What happened? How did you react?

In what ways can you as a group of people become 'a concrete witness of mutual love'? How will other people who are outside of your group see it? What do you need to do?

Worship

LEADER: Jesus said,
RESPONSE: I give you a new commandment:
LEADER: Love one another.
RESPONSE: Love one another.

LEADER:	You must love one another,
RESPONSE:	We must love one another,
LEADER:	Just as I have loved you.
RESPONSE:	Just as you have loved us.
LEADER:	Jesus said,
RESPONSE:	You must love one another just as I have loved you.
LEADER:	It is by your love for one another, that everyone will recognise you as my disciples.
RESPONSE:	It is by our love for one another that everyone will recognise us as your disciples.
LEADER:	Jesus said,
RESPONSE:	I give you a new commandment.
LEADER:	Jesus said,
RESPONSE:	Love one another.

Offer a prayer for the person sitting to your right. Say:

Name . . . Jesus said, 'Love one another.'
May you be recognised as loving. Amen.

Pray this prayer around the group. At the end, join hands
and looking from one to another say:

May the grace of our Lord Jesus Christ, and the love of
God and the fellowship of the Holy Spirit be with us.

Pentecost 12

Getting started
What groups of people do you know who demonstrate a loving
togetherness? What do you admire about them?

Read John 17:20–end.
(Other readings: Isaiah 49:1–6; 2 Corinthians 5:14–6:2.)
20 I pray not only for these
but also for those
who through their teaching will come to believe in me.

21   May they all be one,
     just as, Father, you are in me and I am in you,
     so that they may also be in us,
     so that the world may believe it was you who sent me.
22   I have given them the glory you gave to me,
     that they may be one as we are one.
23   With me in them and you in me,
     may they be so perfected in unity
     that the world will recognise that it was you who sent me
     and that you have loved them as you loved me.
24   Father,
     I want those you have given me
     to be with me where I am,
     so that they may always see my glory
     which you have given me
     because you loved me
     before the foundation of the world.
25   Father, Upright One,
     the world has not known you,
     but I have known you,
     and these have known
     that you have sent me.
26   I have made your name known to them
     and will continue to make it known,
     so that the love with which you loved me may be in them,
     and so that I may be in them.

Comment

In the end it is down to prayer. Jesus had been 'an example'
for the disciples of love, service and solidarity in the face of
opposition. Jesus offers the unity between him and God, the
Father, as a further example to the disciples, and seeks God's
help to unite the disciples 'so that the world may believe it was
you who sent me' (v. 21). John's Gospel focuses upon the
invitation to receive 'eternal life' (John 3:36; 5:24; 6:40, 47);
'And eternal life is this, to know you, the only true God, and

Jesus Christ whom you have sent' (v. 3). Eternal life is based
on faith, not in the after-life. It is a relationship made possible
by Jesus between people of faith and God. It is a relationship
that allows them to live above the enticements of status, power,
wealth and influence for the sake of others.

This is not just for the individual. Unity is something
achieved together and is for the community of disciples. Having
experienced betrayal and disagreements within his own community, Jesus recognises both the problem and the necessity of
a united witness (v. 21). There is an almost mystical power
about such a community, because it is a living demonstration
of the nature of God (vv. 21-3) who is united: Creator, Saviour,
Life-giving Spirit. This quality of unity is like 'a new creation'
where 'the old order is gone and a new being is there to see'
(2 Corinthians 5:17).

For a community of people to live in harmony calls for
constant attention to the task of keeping unity. It is important,
therefore, that there should be a reason for that unity. The
purpose of unity is the furtherance of God's mission – 'so that
the world may believe' (v. 21). 'The ultimate expression of
Jesus' mission is to share God's name, in order to fill people
with God's love. God's name is not money or militarism or
macho. It is the One Who Is, the one upon whom the foundation of the world rests, the one whose love permeates all
that lives and calls it to bear fruit, fruit that will last into eternal
life.'[25]

John, in interpreting Jesus to a community under threat,
wants them to understand that having unity, being bound
together in the love which is given by the Father and Jesus,
makes a clear and hopeful statement to a world where distrust,
deceit and destruction hold sway. People under persecution
today often tell moving and powerful stories of how their
oneness has transformed situations. The Jesuit, Jon Sobrino,
tells of an El Salvadoran woman whose sons had been killed
and daughters gang-raped, yet who spoke of her forgiveness
of the perpetrators; while in the same community, another

woman who had experienced similar tragedy, when challenged
to forgive, said, 'Father, I will try.'

Talking Points

Eternal life is about a relationship between God and people
of faith. It is to be a relationship that enables people to share
the mission of God's love. It is a relationship that allows people
to live above the enticements of status, power, wealth and
influence for the sake of others. How does your community or
church reflect this unity? Give examples. Where could it do
better?

Reflection and Action

How can you as a group share your faith 'so that the world
will recognise' that it was God who sent Jesus to bring forgiveness, hope and a new commandment by which to live?

Worship

LEADER: Jesus prayed:
RESPONSE: May they all be one,
LEADER: just as, Father, you are in me and I am in you
RESPONSE: so that they may also be in us,
LEADER: that the world may believe it was you who sent
            me,
RESPONSE: so that the world may recognise that it was you
            who sent me.
LEADER: Jesus said:
RESPONSE: Father, you have loved them as you loved me.

Read: John 17:20-end.

Concluding **prayer**:

LEADER: Jesus said, Father, Upright One, I have known
            you.
RESPONSE: Thank you, Jesus, that you are one in the Father,
            and the Father is in you.

LEADER: Jesus said, Father, Upright One, these have
               known that you have sent me.

RESPONSE: Thank you, Father, Upright One, that we have
               known that you have sent Jesus.

LEADER: Jesus said, I have made your name known to
               them.

RESPONSE: Thank you that we know your name, Upright
               One, Father.

LEADER: Jesus said, I want those you have given to be
               with me.

RESPONSE: Thank you, Father, Upright One, that the love
               with which you loved Jesus may be in us. Amen.

Pentecost 13

Getting started

Have you ever been persuaded to do something good without
fully recognising all the consequences? Share your experiences.

Read John 16:1–15.
(Other readings: Isaiah 50:4–9; Acts 7:54–8:1.)

1   I have told you all this
     so that you may not fall away.

2   They will expel you from the synagogues,
     and indeed the time is coming
     when anyone who kills you will think he is
     doing a holy service to God.

3   They will do these things
     because they have never known either the Father or me.

4   But I have told you all this,
     so that when the time for it comes
     you may remember that I told you.
     I did not tell you this from the beginning,
     because I was with you;

5   but now I am going to the one who sent me.
     Not one of you asks, 'Where are you going?'

6   Yet you are sad at heart because I have told you this.

7   Still, I am telling you the truth:
      it is for your own good that I am going,
      because unless I go,
      the Paraclete will not come to you;
      but if I go,
      I will send him to you.

8   And when he comes,
      he will show the world how wrong it was,
      about sin,
      and about who was in the right,
      and about judgement:

9   about sin:
      in that they refuse to believe in me;

10   about who was in the right:
      in that I am going to the Father
      and you will see me no more;

11   about judgement:
      in that the prince of this world is already condemned.

12   I still have many things to say to you
      but they would be too much for you to bear now.

13   However, when the Spirit of truth comes
      he will lead you to the complete truth,
      since he will not be speaking of his own accord,
      but will say only what he has been told;
      and he will reveal to you the things to come.

14   He will glorify me,
      since all he reveals to you
      will be taken from what is mine.

15   Everything the Father has is mine;
      that is what I said:
      all he reveals to you
      will be taken from what is mine.

Comment

'You will be expelled' and 'anyone who kills you will think he
is doing a holy service to God' (vv. 1–2). Nowhere in the
Gospel does Jesus put more starkly the risks of following him.
'I did not tell you this from the beginning,' Jesus confesses,
'because I was with you' (v. 4). He gives three reasons why he
is telling them now: firstly, 'so that you will not fall away' (v.
1). Secondly, so 'that when the time comes for them to do
these things, you will remember that I told you' (v. 4). Thirdly,
Jesus says, 'I still have many things to say to you, but they
would be too much for you to bear now' (v. 12). Given that he
has warned them to expect expulsion and execution, it is hard
to imagine what else they would have to bear!

Jesus is concerned about how self-absorbed the disciples are.
For several chapters in John, Jesus has been explaining what
will happen to him (John 13–16), and what he prays for them
(John 17). He has promised them 'the Spirit of truth, who
issues from the Father' (15:26). 'Not one of you asks, "Where
are you going?" Yet you are sad at heart because I have told
you this' (vv. 4–5). It would be easy to judge the disciples as
not caring about Jesus, as well as being over-anxious about
the future. 'Most modern disciples have never experienced the
wrenching pain of ostracism or excommunication and fewer
still sacrificial deaths.'[26] People in such situations need reassur-
ance and comfort.

Jesus reassures his disciples in three ways. Firstly, he reminds
them that he is 'going to the Father' (v. 10), and they 'will see
me no more', for 'he had come from God and was returning
to God' (13:3). Secondly, he tells them, 'it is for your own good
that I am going, because unless I go, the Paraclete will not
come to you' (v. 7). Thirdly, with the comfort comes a new
hope, as well as a challenge, for 'when he comes, he will show
the world [the system] how wrong it was, about sin, and about
who was in the right, and about judgement' (v. 8).

The work of the Spirit is the same as that of Jesus. Jesus
brought God's love into the world, to bring people to faith, to

prevent the world's destruction. The Spirit will convict people 'about who was in the right' (v. 9). The Spirit will also convict the world over its misplaced sense of justice, which expels and murders the people of God (vv. 1 and 15). Finally, the Spirit will convince the System of its misjudgement, for example when it sees Jesus as 'demon' (Matthew 11:18) and 'sinner' (Matthew 11:19); and his followers as deserving of excommunication and death.

Jesus reassures his disciples that just as he has been for them, so will the Spirit. As he kept certain things from them until they were able to receive such truths, so will the Spirit. The Spirit will give to the disciples all they need to carry the message of God's truth. Indeed, 'when the Spirit of truth comes, he will lead you to the complete truth' (v. 13).

The *suffering community* is now comforted, reassured, and opened up to new possibilities within the family (Pentecost 14), society (Pentecost 15) and among the neighbours (Pentecost 16).

Talking Points

'If I had known all this, I'd never have joined', might have been an understandable reaction when Jesus said, 'I did not tell you this from the beginning' (v. 4). To what extent do you feel that being a Christian is tougher than you reckoned? How does the Spirit assure and comfort you? Where have been the signs of hope of the Spirit at work in the world? In what ways have you seen the world (the system) convicted over its misplaced sense of justice?

Reflection and Action

This week marks the end of three reflections on community as a place of serving others, witnessing to others, and suffering because of others. How as a group have you served, witnessed and suffered? What have you learned? The next three *Seeds of the Word* reflections are on the *Family*, *Society* and *Neighbours*.

Worship

LEADER:	Jesus said, I have told you all this
PEOPLE:	So that you will not fall away.
INTERCESSOR 1:	For those who are being expelled from their homes:
PEOPLE:	May they not fall away.
INTERCESSOR 2:	For those who are being killed because those doing it think they are serving God:
PEOPLE:	May they not fall away.
INTERCESSOR 3:	For those who do these things, because they have not known the Father or Jesus:
PEOPLE:	Show the system how wrong it is about sin, and about who is in the right and about judgement.
INTERCESSOR 4:	Spirit of truth,
PEOPLE:	Come, lead to the complete truth; Glorify God; Reveal all things; May we not fall away.

Pentecost 14

Getting started

Who was the centre of warmth in your life when you were eight years old? Why was that?

Read Mark 10:2–16.
(Other readings: Proverbs 31:10-end; Ephesians 5:25–6:4.)

2   Some Pharisees approached him and asked, 'Is it lawful for a man to divorce his wife?' They were putting him to the
3   test. He answered them, 'What did Moses command you?'
4   They replied, 'Moses allowed us to draw up a writ of dismissal
5   in cases of divorce.' Then Jesus said to them, 'It was because you were so hard-hearted that he wrote this commandment
6   for you. But from the beginning of creation he made them

7   male and female. This is why a man leaves his father and
8   mother, and the two become one flesh. They are no longer
9   two, therefore, but one flesh. So then, what God has united,
10   human beings must not divide.' Back in the house, the dis-
11   ciples questioned him again about this, and he said to them,
     'Whoever divorces his wife and marries another is guilty of
12   adultery against her. And if a woman divorces her husband
     and marries another she is guilty of adultery too.'

13   People were bringing little children to him, for him to touch
14   them. The disciples scolded them, but when Jesus saw this
     he was indignant and said to them, 'Let the little children
     come to me; do not stop them; for it is to such as these that
15   the kingdom of God belongs. In truth I tell you, anyone who
     does not welcome the kingdom of God like a little child will
16   never enter it.' Then he embraced them, laid his hands on
     them and gave them his blessing.

Comment

The theme of this week is *Family*. It is ironic that the set Gospel
begins with a question to Jesus about divorce! However, given
that in Britain the divorce rate is reckoned to be one in three
marriages, it is certainly topical. Jesus is journeying to Jerusalem with his disciples, and he is constantly put under pressure
by Pharisees, scribes, and other political and religious leaders
who are striving to build their case against him. Some Pharisees
approached him and asked, 'Is it lawful for a man to divorce
his wife?' Jesus replied by asking a question, 'What did Moses
command you?' (v. 3) They replied by saying, in effect, that
women have no reciprocal rights; a husband could divorce his
wife if 'she does not please him because he finds something
objectionable about her' (Deuteronomy 24:1).

Jesus understood the reality that 'in the biblical world,
women can generally be described as someone's property. Until
marriage, a woman is the property of her father; after marriage,
the property of her husband; and as a widow, the property of
her son.'[27] However, Jesus is about making a new order in

human relationships, and he begins with a call for women's rights, reminding them of the creation narrative: 'And God created humankind in God's image, in the image of God he created humankind, male and female' (Genesis 1:27). When 'a man leaves his father and his mother, and cleaves to his woman and they become one flesh,' (Genesis 2:24) the implication is clear, that 'both male and female are responsible for not separating what God has joined together.'[28] In effect, Jesus is confronting the practice of divorce by men for selfish reasons. Women are no longer to be regarded as property, but as having equal dignity as human beings.

In private conversation later with his disciples (vv. 10–12), they want to know the implications of such equality in a society where women were more likely to be publicly accused of adultery than men. If a woman was not 'owned' by a man, she had little option other than to become a prostitute, thereby making her adultery very public (see John 4:16–20; John 8:1–11). To his disciples Jesus says, 'Whoever divorces his wife and marries another is guilty of adultery against her. And if a woman divorces her husband and marries another she is guilty of adultery too' (v. 12). In an equal relationship, the charge of adultery may be made against either husband or wife, if they break their marriage vows. But, as always, Jesus is after something more, and that is that both parties be faithful.

Children in the Gospel are usually pictured as sick or oppressed (see Mark 5:21ff., 7:24ff., 9:14ff.). Even Jesus' disciples regard them as of little consequence (v. 13). Also, they are always victims in divorce situations. Children were to be included in Jesus' vision of new relationships; indeed, their vulnerability was to be the example for everyone who would follow Jesus, 'anyone who does not welcome the kingdom of God like a little child will never enter it' (v. 16).

Talking Points

Jesus had some very hard things to say about family. At one point, he renounced his own family by saying, ' "Who are my mother and my brothers?" And looking at those sitting in a circle round him, he said, "Here are my mother and my brothers. Anyone who does the will of God, that person is my brother and sister and mother" ' (Mark 3:33–5). 'He offers an alternative,' says Walter Wink, 'a new family, made up of those whose delusions have been shattered, who are linked, not by that tightest of all bonds, the blood-tie, but by the doing of God's will.'[29] Why do you think Jesus put 'doing God's will' above blood-ties?

Kinship is the experience of belonging to the human family. All too often, we fail to care for one another as kin – fellow human beings. Why? How could things be different? How should we treat each other as men, women and children? What kind of lives should Christians be living as a model for others?

Reflection and Action

Reflect on your own relationships with husband, wife, partner, children, brothers and sisters. In what ways are you prevented from doing something you believe to be right, or that you would like to do because it would be good for you, because of limitations placed upon you by any of these relationships? Ask yourself, am I squashing the aspirations and hopes of someone to whom I am related because of some fear, or need in me?

Worship

Begin by listening to someone read a child's reflection:

> If God isn't anyone, then maybe we're not, either. At my great aunt's funeral, the minister said, 'ashes to ashes' and I got scared. But if there's no God, that's all there is – ashes. No heaven, no hell. If God is someone, then we're someone, too. He'll make us someone, if we let Him. I hope He will – that's what you pray for: that He'll be something for you, if you've given Him a chance, by being mostly good. You can't be all good, I know.[30]

Keep a few minutes of silence. Try and recall the earliest thought you had about God. Share it with the group.

After all have shared, take a few minutes' more silence. Do you recall the first prayer you learned as a child/adult? Remember: 'Gentle Jesus, meek and mild, look upon a little child. Pity my simplicity and help me to come to thee.' Offer your first prayer in the group.

Close:

> 'In truth, anyone who does not welcome the Kingdom of God like a little child will never enter it.'

Pentecost 15

Getting started

Have you ever taken part in a demonstration, street protest, or strike? What was it about? Why did you take part?

Read Matthew 22:15–22.
(Other readings: Isaiah 45:1–7; Romans 13:1–7.)

15 **Then the Pharisees went away to work out between them**
16 **how to trap him in what he said. And they sent their disciples to him, together with some Herodians, to say, 'Master, we know that you are an honest man and teach the way of God in all honesty, and that you are not afraid of anyone, because**
17 **human rank means nothing to you. Give us your opinion,**
18 **then. Is it permissible to pay taxes to Caesar or not?' But Jesus was aware of their malice and replied, 'You hypocrites!**
19 **Why are you putting me to the test? Show me the money**
20 **you pay the tax with.' They handed him a denarius, and he**
21 **said, 'Whose portrait is this? Whose title?' They replied, 'Caesar's.' Then he said to them, 'Very well, pay Caesar what**
22 **belongs to Caesar – and God what belongs to God.' When they heard this they were amazed; they left him alone and went away.**

Comment

'There are only two things certain in life: death and taxes,' someone once cynically remarked. Tax, as in most countries, was a hot issue. Throughout the first seventy years of the Christian era in Palestine the imposition of high taxes by surrogates of the Roman Empire, such as Herod, often led the peasantry, upon whom the burden of taxes fell, into revolt. Non-payment was the mildest act of civil disobedience. Always there was retribution. Small holders would have their land expropriated, and imprisonment was often mandatory.

Jesus, who was born during a census to determine tax rates (Luke 2:1–3), is asked his opinion about paying tax to the emperor of Rome, Caesar. Jesus is in a 'no win' situation. If he says, 'Yes, pay', he will lose face among those who have been offering him support. If he says, 'No, don't pay', the Roman authorities can legally take action against him. Jesus sees the plot, and 'deftly escapes the political trap by turning the political challenge back upon his opponents, refusing to commit himself unless and until they do.'[31]

By asking his challengers to identify whose head is on the coin, Jesus is at once testing their allegiance, while refusing to reveal his own. They reply, 'Caesar's' – the coin would also have borne the phrase 'August and Divine Son'. For many patriotic Jews to be in possession of such a coin was an act of betrayal. But Jesus replies, 'Repay the one to whom you are indebted.' Put another way, 'If you are indebted to Caesar, pay him his due; if you are indebted to God, pay what is due to God.' In Matthew's and Mark's Gospels, this discussion follows Jesus' deeply subversive parable about 'the wicked tenants' who try to steal from God what rightfully belongs to him (Matthew 21:33–46; Mark 12:1–12).

Jesus chooses the path of non-alignment with either position, because quite simply he regards everything as on loan from God. 'What is God's' is stipulated in the vineyard parable – all leaders are only tenants. This text, about 'paying to Caesar

what is Caesar's and to God what is God's' is frequently quoted
out of context in support for the *status quo*, or to back up the
doctrine of being obedient citizens in *society*. Jesus sees 'what
is God's' as covering everything. Humanity has on loan the
earth, temporal power and leadership.

By refusing to line up against Caesar, Jesus again indicates
to his disciples that they should not look to him as a Messiah
who will take political power. However, Jesus does encourage
them to 'live faithfully in society, according to that society's
legitimate and just rules, always recognising Jesus' ultimate
primacy over Caesar. All reigns on earth exist under the reign
of this God-with-us.'[32]

Talking Points

Have you ever been in a 'no win' situation? How did you
resolve it? Share your experience with the group. Are there
occasions when civil disobedience is legitimate? How do we
decide what belongs to God in our lives?

Worship

Listen to this account from a French Protestant community in
the Second World War:

> French Jews were being rounded up and sent to concen-
> tration camps. One village, under its pastor, André
> Trocmé, resisted, hiding Jews throughout the war. 'We do
> not know what a Jew is: we only know men', he told the
> authorities. One day, a sermon was being preached on
> 'everyone is to obey the governing authorities' (Romans
> 13). To anyone who knew the chapter, and the people of
> Le Chambon knew it well, the ethic of neighbourly love –
> 'You shall love your neighbour as yourself' – demanded
> not a bitter confrontation with the government, but a
> perfunctory minimal respect for the 'governing authori-
> ties', with a firm, but quiet hint that there are limits to

that respect, limits set by the commandment not to do wrong to a neighbour.[33]

Keep silence for a few moments. Who, in this week's news, has been wronged by the authorities? Ask each person to share the example that comes to mind.

Keep a few more minutes' silence, then ask each person to repeat their concern and all say after each one:

ALL: Love can cause no harm to your neighbour, so love is
        the fulfilment of the Law.
        Give to God what belongs to God.

Conclude with the Lord's Prayer.

Pentecost 16

Getting started
Who would you regard as your neighbour? Just the person who lives next door? Who else?

Read Luke 10:25–37.
(Other readings: Leviticus 19:9–18; Romans 12:9-end.)

25 And now a lawyer stood up and, to test him, asked, 'Master,
26 what must I do to inherit eternal life?' He said to him, 'What
27 is written in the Law? What is your reading of it?' He replied,
'You must love the Lord your God with all your heart, with
all your soul, with all your strength, and with all your mind,
28 and your neighbour as yourself.' Jesus said to him, 'You have
answered right, do this and life is yours.'

29   But the man was anxious to justify himself and said to
30 Jesus, 'And who is my neighbour?' In answer Jesus said, 'A
man was once on his way down from Jerusalem to Jericho
and fell into the hands of bandits; they stripped him, beat
31 him and then made off, leaving him half dead. Now a priest
happened to be travelling down the same road, but when he
32 saw the man, he passed by on the other side. In the same

way a Levite who came to the place saw him, and passed by
33 on the other side. But a Samaritan traveller who came on
34 him was moved with compassion when he saw him. He went
up to him and bandaged his wounds, pouring oil and wine
on them. He then lifted him onto his own mount and took
35 him to an inn and looked after him. Next day he took out
two denarii and handed them to the innkeeper and said,
"Look after him, and on my way back I will make good any
36 extra expense you have." Which of these three, do you think,
proved himself a neighbour to the man who fell into the
37 bandits' hands?' He replied, 'The one who showed pity
towards him.' Jesus said to him, 'Go, and do the same
yourself.'

Comment

'Don't ignore the dialogue!' might well be the instruction that
should be given to all readers of this parable. This is not simply
a story about reaching out to people in need. 'The parable is
not a pleasant tale about the traveller who did his good deed:
it is a damning indictment of social, racial, and religious superiority.'[34] The lawyer wants to *do* something to 'inherit eternal
life' (v. 26) and he wants to 'justify himself' (v. 29). As a lawyer,
the man knows that only those who are legally entitled can
inherit anything. As a Jew, he understands that his forebears
inherited the land of promise. 'This inheritance is understood
as a gift of God. Israel does nothing to either deserve it or
achieve it.'[35] Eternal life was understood as possessing the land,
and the way 'to inherit eternal life' (v. 26) was to keep the
Law. The lawyer knows 'to love God and neighbour' is the Law,
but the question is, 'who is my neighbour?' Or, to put it another
way, are there any limits as to who should be regarded as
neighbour? By tradition, there were limits on who was
regarded as neighbour. Both Jews and Samaritans were people
of the Law of Moses, and they saw their neighbours as kinsfolk
and those of the same ethnic and religious origin.

Against this understanding, Jesus tells the story of the robbers, the victim and the rescuer. If he had been telling a simple 'good neighbour story', he could have spoken of a well-meaning Jew helping a Samaritan. But in Luke's Gospel, Jesus is pictured as one who is concerned to heal the deepest wounds between peoples, and Jews and Samaritans were the bitterest of enemies; their animosity was deeply historical and as fresh as yesterday's atrocity. During Jesus' childhood, Samaritans had desecrated the Temple in Jerusalem; and in 48 AD Jews had killed and mutilated a whole village in Galilee. Luke tells three stories about Samaritans, while Matthew and Mark give no such detail (Luke 9:51–6; Luke 17:11–19; Luke 10:25–37).

Jesus describes the Samaritan traveller as 'moved with compassion'; he has a gut-level concern for the victim of violence. Such an idea would have been anathema to devout Jews. Jesus is being deeply provocative, for his mission is to break down traditional barriers, old enmities. The impact of such a story on the lawyer and the other listeners would not have been lost. Jesus was saying, in effect, 'Be neighbour to anyone in need, express compassion, even to your enemies. This is the goal of those who want to receive eternal life. It remains a gift, but it can be aspired to by giving unexpected love to the most unexpected of people.'

Talking Points

Samaritans and Jews experienced conflict that was in part ethnic and religious, and the result of accumulated animosities over centuries. What modern-day examples can you think of that parallel this conflict? Whom would you describe as 'Samaritans' in your country? Why do you think religious and racial bigotry is so difficult to overcome? So often in ethnic or religious conflict it is easy to 'blame' those who oppose us. How should Christians deal with this kind of situation?

Reflection and Action

What experience of prejudice do you have? How are you prejudiced? Try and identify areas where you as a group are prejudiced. What can you do to overcome prejudice or bigotry in yourself, your family, your neighbourhood, church or city?

Worship
Keep silence for a few moments. Recall an occasion when you were 'a Good Samaritan' to someone; or they were to you.

Reread the Good Samaritan story – Luke 10:25–37. Tell your own Good Samaritan story. After each person has told their story, pray:

> Lord, let our love be without pretence. Make us joyful in hope and open to sharing with anyone in need.

Conclude by saying:

> Holy God,
> whose name is not honoured
> where the needy are not served
> and the powerless are treated with contempt:
> may we embrace our neighbour
> with the same tenderness
> that we ourselves require;
> so your justice may be fulfilled in love
> through Jesus Christ. Amen.[36]

Celebrate – Plan an informal meal, and invite people who might be interested in knowing about your group.

The next series in *Seeds of the Word* is on *Faith*. There are four sessions. Plan how you are going to meet, and where and when.

Pentecost 17

Getting started
What is the most unexpected kindness that you have received? Who was it from? Why was it so unexpected?

Read Luke 17:11–19.
(Other readings: Jeremiah 7:1–11; James 1:16-end.)

11   **Now it happened that on the way to Jerusalem he was travel-**
12   **ling in the borderlands of Samaria and Galilee. As he entered**
      one of the villages, ten men suffering from a virulent skin
13   **disease came to meet him. They stood some way off and**
14   **called to him, 'Jesus! Master! Take pity on us.' When he saw**
      them he said, 'Go and show yourselves to the priests.' Now
15   **as they were going away they were cleansed. Finding himself**
      cured, one of them turned back praising God at the top of
16   **his voice and threw himself prostrate at the feet of Jesus and**
17   **thanked him. The man was a Samaritan. This led Jesus to**
      say, 'Were not all ten made clean? The other nine, where are
18   **they? It seems that no one has come back to give praise to**
19   **God, except this foreigner.' And he said to the man, 'Stand**
      up and go on your way. Your faith has saved you.'

Comment

This is a story about faith rather than healing. It is a story that
has parallels in other Gospels (see Matthew 8:1–4 and Mark
1:40–5. It is worth noting too Luke 5:12–16.) Luke may well
have taken the story of the healing of the leper, and added the
presence of 'a Samaritan' (v. 16).

    Jewish tradition required that anyone claiming to be cured
of skin disease should present themselves to the priests at the
Temple and make the offering, or sacrifice prescribed by
the Law of Moses. When the ten skin-disease sufferers are
healed, Jesus, in Luke's account, sends them to 'the priests' (v.
14). In this account, Luke does not record Jesus requiring that
they make a sacrifice. Why? We know that Luke was particularly concerned in his Gospel to heal the wounds of animosity
between Jews and Samaritans (see *Comment Pentecost 16*). 'We
may ask whether this was out of courtesy and sympathy for
the one Samaritan. His temple had been brutally destroyed
by the Jew, Hyrcanus, in 129 BC. Therefore he could not offer
sacrifice. His nine companions go to Jerusalem to Herod's

Temple. The Samaritan returns to give thanks to the new
temple, Jesus.'[37]

Luke gives three Samaritan stories to emphasise his commitment to reconciliation between peoples (Luke 9:51–6; Luke
10:25–37; Luke 17:11–19). Only John's Gospel tells another
Samaritan story (John 4:1–42). This is about a Samaritan
woman, a double outcast to Jewish hearers. Jesus invites the
Samaritan woman, almost certainly a prostitute (John 4:18–19)
to become a 'true worshipper' of God (John 4:23) and 'worship
the Father in spirit and truth' (John 4:23–4). The healed Samaritan leper who came back 'praising God at the top of his voice'
(Luke 19:15) was one such 'true worshipper'.

Luke, who also wrote the Book of Acts, records how the first
church to form outside Jerusalem was in fact among Samaritans
(Acts 8). His record of Jesus' commitment to the Samaritan
'enemy' gives evidence of reconciliation between Samaritans
and Jews. Philip, one of the apostles 'proclaimed Christ to
them' (Acts 8:5); then Peter and John came from the Jerusalem
church, 'went down there [to Samaria] and prayed for them to
receive the Holy Spirit . . . they laid their hands on them, and
they received the Holy Spirit' (Acts 8:14,17). 'Without the
dramatic removal of the ancient and bitter barriers between
the two . . . the young church of God would have been in
schism from the very inception of its mission.'[38]

Talking Points
How has your faith in Jesus Christ helped you to overcome
prejudice in your own heart and mind? How did this happen?
Where is reconciliation necessary in the life of your church? If
Luke were writing for your church, what group would he ident-
ify as being like Samaritans? Why?

Reflection and Action
Having identified where reconciliation is necessary in your
church, what steps can you take as a community to bring

healing and reconciliation? Plan out your ideas, and set tasks for people.

Worship
Use the Liturgy for Reconciliation on page 239.

For next week plan some prayers, readings and songs on the theme of *Faith*.

Pentecost 18

Getting started
What makes you envious of other people?

Read Matthew 5:17–26.
(Other readings: Deuteronomy 26:1–11; 2 Corinthians 8:1–9.)

17 'Do not imagine that I have come to abolish the Law or the Prophets. I have come not to abolish but to complete them.

18 In truth I tell you, till heaven and earth disappear, not one dot, not one little stroke, is to disappear from the Law until

19 all its purpose is achieved. Therefore, anyone who infringes even one of the least of these commandments and teaches others to do the same will be considered the least in the kingdom of Heaven; but the person who keeps them and teaches them will be considered great in the kingdom of Heaven.

20   'For I tell you, if your uprightness does not surpass that of the scribes and Pharisees, you will never get into the kingdom of Heaven.

21   'You have heard how it was said to our ancestors, *You shall not kill*; and if anyone does kill he must answer for it before

22 the court. But I say this to you, anyone who is angry with a brother will answer for it before the court; anyone who calls a brother "Fool" will answer for it before the Sanhedrin and anyone who calls him "Traitor" will answer for it in hell fire.

23 So then, if you are bringing your offering to the altar and there remember that your brother has something against you,

24 **leave your offering there before the altar, go and be rec-**
       onciled with your brother first, and then come back and
25 **present your offering. Come to terms with your opponent in**
       good time while you are still on the way to the court with
       him, or he may hand you over to the judge and the judge to
26 **the officer, and you will be thrown into prison. In truth I tell**
       you, you will not get out until you have paid the last penny.'

Comment

Jesus was a Jew – a person of the Book. Jews believe that God
is revealed in both deed and word – the written Word, the Law
of Moses or the *Torah*. Jesus was a teacher, a *rabbi*, steeped in
the Scriptures. He understood the intimate details of practising
Jewish faith, the 'tithe [percentage of a crop] of mint, dill and
cummin' and the 'weightier matters of the Law – justice, mercy,
good faith!' (Matthew 23:23) For Jews, discerning truth is all
important. This faith search is often carried out through discussion and argument. As passages of Scripture are read, so
teachers, rabbis, seek to discern its truth.

Matthew 5 contains a series of Jesus' teachings, often
referred to as 'The Sermon on the Mount'. In these teachings,
Jesus takes a number of significant phrases from Jewish tradition and seeks to make them clear from his perspective. He
does not set out to contradict but elucidate, 'Do not imagine
that I have come to abolish the Law or the Prophets. I have
come not to abolish them but to complete them' (v. 17). If
Jesus had meant to 'abolish the Law', he would have argued
differently. For instance, 'when Jesus says, "You heard . . . you
should not kill" (5:21), an antithesis would run, "but I say to
you, do away with anyone who stands in your way." '[39] But
Jesus doesn't say that, he builds on the meaning of the Law,
'You have heard how it was said to our ancestors, *You shall
not kill* . . . But I say this to you, anyone who is angry with a
brother will answer for it' (v. 21).

Jesus wants his hearers to go beyond the 'dos and don'ts' of
the ethical teachings of the ancestors and says, in effect, 'not

only murder, but even anger is condemned; not only adultery, but even a lewd glance is illicit; not only perjury, but any oath is evil; not only peaceableness, but also humility and renunciation of rights are building blocks of the shalom of the future.'[40] In the mind of Jesus, the community can only exist in *shalom* – peace and harmony – if not only the prohibitions to sin are kept (Do not kill, do not steal, etc.), but also the desire to sin is resisted too. The Tenth Commandment says, 'You shall not set your heart on your neighbour's house' ... and other property (Exodus 20:17). It is the envy, the consuming desire to possess, that Jesus recognises as the cause of sin. The 'uprightness that surpasses that of the scribes and Pharisees' (v. 20) is a community life lived without hatred, anger, or envy, in a relationship going beyond the demands of mere justice.

In the Jewish tradition, the Day of Atonement is the holiest day of the year. It is a day when two acts of reconciliation are required to take place: one between humans and God, and the other between human beings who are in dispute. 'So then if you are bringing your offering to the altar ... and there remember your brother has something against you, leave ... go and be reconciled with your brother and then ... present your offering' (vv. 24–5). It is much easier to confess sin in a meeting than to re-establish right relationships with people whom you have offended, or have offended you, says Jesus. But 'you will never get into the kingdom of Heaven' (v. 20) unless reconciliation is made between you and others, *as well as* between you and God.

Talking Points
Why is it so difficult for people to re-establish right relationships with people whom they have offended, or have offended them? Why do you think Jesus was so insistent that reconciliation between people should be made as well as between individuals and God? Is it possible in our church or community life to live without hatred, anger or envy? Why do you think that Jesus was anxious to nip sin in the bud by saying so clearly

over issues such as murder, adultery, coveting other people's possessions – 'Don't even think about it'?

Reflection and Action
Share any progress made in the work of reconciliation you agreed upon last week. Has today's reflection given you any insights into your work of reconciliation? At a personal level, are there areas where you need to be re-establishing right relationships? Do you need a *mediator*? Whom will you ask?

Worship
Offer your worship on the theme of *Faith*.

For next time plan an act of worship on the theme of *Set your hearts on God's saving justice* (Matthew 6:33).

Pentecost 19

Getting started
Who is the freest spirit you have ever known? What did you admire about them? What caused you greatest anxiety about their lifestyle?

Read Matthew 6:24-end.
(Other readings: Genesis 28:10-end; Hebrews 11:1–2, 8–16.)

24 **'No one can be the slave of two masters: he will either hate the first and love the second, or be attached to the first and despise the second. You cannot be the slave both of God and money.**

25 **'That is why I am telling you not to worry about your life and what you are to eat, nor about your body, and what you are to wear. Surely life is more than food, and the body more**

26 **than clothing! Look at the birds in the sky. They do not sow or reap or gather into barns; yet your heavenly Father feeds**

27 **them. Are you not worth much more than they are? Can any of you, however much you worry, add one single cubit to your**

28 **span of life? And why worry about clothing? Think of the**

flowers growing in the fields; they never have to work or spin;
29 yet I assure you that not even Solomon in all his royal robes
30 was clothed like one of these. Now if that is how God clothes
the wild flowers growing in the field which are there today
and thrown into the furnace tomorrow, will he not much more
31 look after you, you who have so little faith? So do not worry;
do not say, "What are we to eat? What are we to drink?
32 What are we to wear?" It is the gentiles who set their hearts
on all these things. Your heavenly Father knows you need
33 them all. Set your hearts on his kingdom first, and on God's
saving justice, and all these other things will be given you as
34 well. So do not worry about tomorrow: tomorrow will take
care of itself. Each day has enough trouble of its own.'

Comment

'I am telling you not to worry about your life . . .' (v. 25). Jesus
poses a challenge to his followers who are caught between
anxiety, 'What are we to eat? What are we to drink? What are
we to wear?' (v. 31), and faith. 'Eating', 'drinking', 'wearing'
are essential elements of human life, but Jesus is concerned to
put them into a right perspective. 'No one', he says, 'can be
the slave of two masters . . . You cannot be the slave both of
God and money' (v. 24). The word used for slave here means
'one who serves', or 'one who is given over to something' in
the way an addict is given over to their addiction. Jesus recognised that money was addictive, and therefore what it could
buy was addictive too. 'Wherever your treasure is, there will
your heart be too' (6:21).

Jesus indicates that the 'domination free order of God'[41]
begins for people when they discover what preoccupies them;
to what they are 'given over' and 'addicted'. Because money
produces inequality, Jesus calls for his communities of faith to
be people who recognise their addiction and relocate where
their treasure is by setting their hearts on 'God's saving justice'
(v. 33). Jesus challenges the 'religionist's dream of being able
to be "spiritual" and still amass wealth within an unjust system.

Jesus pronounces an unconditional "no": "You cannot serve God and wealth." '[42]

There is a realism to Jesus' radicalism. He wants the new order to begin now. He holds to the view that the earth will provide for the needs of all humanity, provided people act justly by sharing equally. Jesus says, in effect, that just as God feeds the birds with what they need, so will the earth God created feed you, who are infinitely more valuable than the birds. Your part in it is to have a 'hunger and thirst for justice' (5:6) and to refuse to worry about tomorrow by taking 'one day at a time'. 'One day at a time' is the core of the 'recovery programme' for those working to overcome addictions. 'At its heart, a recovery programme is essentially a programme for conversion.'[43]

Matthew's Gospel is addressed to increasingly affluent Christian communities who are becoming obsessed with their wealth and how to use it (v. 30). Jesus directs them to 'hunger and thirst' (5:6) for 'God's saving justice' (v. 33), in order that 'you who have so little faith' (v. 31) may, through letting each day 'take care of itself' (v. 34), find their faith strengthened.

Talking Points
Jesus believed possessions, particularly money, led to injustice and were unfair. Do you agree? Jesus commended people for selling their surplus possessions and giving the proceeds to the disadvantaged. Was he laying an unrealistic expectation on people?

What are the things in life that worry you? To what are you 'given over' or 'addicted'? Jesus called his followers 'to hunger and thirst for God's saving justice'. Matthew seems to suggest that it is too big a task to do other than on a day by day basis. Our addictions prevent us from serving God's cause 'first'. To 'break the habit', we need to find ways each day of giving up an area of injustice in our lives, and 'seeking justice'.

Reflection and Action

In what ways can you encourage each other 'not to worry
about your life'? Having identified the things that worry you
and to which you are addicted, can you agree strategies to help
one another to 'break the habit'?

Share any ongoing experience of re-establishing right
relationships since your last meeting.

Worship

Offer your worship on the theme *Set your hearts on God's
saving justice.*

For next time bring some candles and ask each person in the
group to offer a prayer of thanksgiving for the re-establishing
of a relationship. This can be either personal, or someone you
know, or an item from the news. As you offer the prayer, light
the candle and say:

> For the remaking of this relationship
> thanks be to God.

Pentecost 20

Getting started

When in your life have you been most tempted to retaliate
against someone who did you, or someone else, wrong?

Read Luke 9:51-end.
(Other readings: Daniel 3:13–26; Romans 8:18–25.)

51   Now it happened that as the time drew near for him to be
      taken up, he resolutely turned his face towards Jerusalem
52   and sent messengers ahead of him. These set out, and they
      went into a Samaritan village to make preparation for him,
53   but the people would not receive him because he was
54   making for Jerusalem. Seeing this, the disciples James and
      John said, 'Lord, do you want us to call down fire from

55, 56 heaven to burn them up?' But he turned and rebuked them,
• and they went on to another village.

57   As they travelled along, they met a man on the road who
58   said to him, 'I will follow you wherever you go.' Jesus
answered, 'Foxes have holes and the birds of the air have
nests, but the Son of man has nowhere to lay his head.'

59   Another to whom he said, 'Follow me,' replied, 'Let me
60   go and bury my father first.' But he answered, 'Leave the
dead to bury their dead; your duty is to go and spread
the news of the kingdom of God.'

61   Another said, 'I will follow you, sir, but first let me go
62   and say good-bye to my people at home.' Jesus said to him,
'Once the hand is laid on the plough, no one who looks
back is fit for the kingdom of God.'

Comment

'Live simply' is Jesus' directive for all those who are inclined
to worry about life (Luke 12:22–34). Practising what he
preached, Jesus recalls, 'Foxes have holes and the birds of the
air have nests, but the Son of man has nowhere to lay his head'
(v. 58). This is not a statement designed to get people feeling
sorry for him, but a reminder of the commitment necessary to
bring about real change in the *status quo*. Jesus is even prepared
to encourage the violation of religious duty. To the man whose
father is dying, he says somewhat crudely, 'Leave the dead to
bury their dead; your duty is to go and spread the news of the
kingdom of God' (v. 60).

As Jesus and his party journey towards Jerusalem, they pass
through a Samaritan village which, contrary to the culture of
the time, refuses to give them hospitality. 'Of course, Jews do
not associate with Samaritans' (John 4:10), and the party is
headed for Jerusalem which for Samaritans was alien territory,
so perhaps this is no great surprise. Among Jesus' disciples are
James and John, called the 'sons of rage' (Mark 3:17). They
are indignant and prejudiced against Samaritans; they believe
that some act of retaliation should follow, and ask Jesus, 'do

you want us to call down fire from heaven to burn them up?'
(v. 54) Jesus tells them off and, in a text which is in many
manuscripts and in the footnotes of the *New Jerusalem Bible*,
among others, says: 'You do not know what spirit you are made
of. The Son of man came not to destroy souls, but to save
them.'

In repudiating violence, Jesus is challenging the law of retaliation. The history of the Jews and Samaritans had been one of
violence and counter-violence. Jesus both opposed evil and
sought to build a society of justice for *all* peoples. In Luke's
Gospel, as we noted during Pentecost 16 and 17, the Samaritans
receive particular attention from Jesus. The traditional 'enemy',
they have been responsible for many evil acts against Jews.
Jesus sees no merit in continuing this 'tit for tat', but repeats
the Golden Rule – 'Do to others as you would have them do
to you' (Matthew 7:12; Luke 6:31).

Luke wrote his Gospel in a period of heightened tension
between the two communities. In the year 51 AD some Samaritans murdered a Jew in a village called Ginae. When the news
was received in Jerusalem, an enraged mob entered the village
and massacred men, women and children in retaliation. This
event nearly led to a civil war. By highlighting the mission of
Jesus to the Samaritans, Luke was gently applying pressure to
his readers to recall the teaching of non-violence offered by
Jesus. Also, by planting the story of the hardships involved in
being faithful to Christ (vv. 57–62), he was reminding them just
what a difficult and costly alternative following the way of
Jesus was.

It is relatively easy to 'love enemies', 'pray for those who
persecute you' and 'forgive one another from the heart' when
life is normal, but when historic animosity is revived in a time
of heightened tension, making such choices becomes more
difficult and costly.

Talking Points

Luke invites his readers to recall Jesus' attitude of non-violence. He reminded them of the directive to 'love your enemies', 'pray for those who persecute you' and 'forgive one another from the heart'. Is such teaching appropriate for us today? How? Why? What makes it so difficult to do what Jesus said?

Reflection and Action

Share your successes and failure in overcoming your 'addictions' since you last met. Also reflect on the process of seeking reconciliation, either personally, or in your church and community. Who are the 'enemies' you are 'to love'? How can you support and encourage each other in 'loving', 'praying for' and 'forgiving from the heart' those whom you have identified as needing this grace from you?

Worship

Offer your acts of thanksgiving for the *remaking of relationships*. Light your candle as you offer your prayer and say:

> For the remaking of this relationship
> thanks be to God.

Next week marks the beginning of Pentecost Unit 6. This is the final unit in this season. Plan three sessions of *Seeds of the Word* on the themes:

> *Hoping*
> *Choosing*
> *Waiting*

Pentecost 21

Getting started
What is it that you hope most for in the world?

Read Luke 18:1–8.
(Other readings: Habakkuk 2:1–4; Acts 26:1–8.)

1   Then he told them a parable about the need to pray continu-
2   ally and never lose heart. 'There was a judge in a certain
     town,' he said, 'who had neither fear of God nor respect for
3   anyone. In the same town there was also a widow who kept
     on coming to him and saying, "I want justice from you against
4   my enemy!" For a long time he refused, but at last he said
     to himself, "Even though I have neither fear of God nor
5   respect for any human person, I must give this widow her
     just rights since she keeps pestering me, or she will come and
     slap me in the face." '
6   And the Lord said, 'You notice what the unjust judge has
7   to say? Now will not God see justice done to his elect if they
     keep calling to him day and night even though he still delays
8   to help them? I promise you, he will see justice done to them,
     and done speedily. But when the Son of man comes, will he
     find any faith on earth?'

Comment

This story reveals two things: the difficulty of getting justice,
and the need to pray. The scenario is a widow, probably poor,
for some reason being denied justice by a judge. The judge,
described as having 'neither fear of God nor respect for
anyone' (v. 2), does not want to make judgement, perhaps
because he has received no bribes. By not making a judgement,
he seems to favour her opponent, maybe *he* has offered bribes.
The dispute between the widow and the judge is very public.
In Middle Eastern culture, women can shout what they like at
opponents but cannot be touched unless they commit violence.
Clearly the judge fears violence, and it is this that causes him
to give in to her demands: 'I must give this widow her just
rights since she keeps pestering me, or she will come and slap
me in the face' (v. 5).

In Luke's Gospel, Jesus recognises the difficulty widows have
in receiving justice on two occasions. He criticises the scribes

'who devour the property of widows' (Luke 20:47) while offering 'long prayers', and 'taking the best seats in the synagogue
and the places of honour at banquets'. Against this background,
Jesus promises all who suffer injustice and cry out to God that
'he will see justice done . . . and done speedily' (v. 8). But Jesus
says God cannot bring justice without the prayers of his people:
'will not God see justice done to his elect if they keep calling
to him day and night . . .'.

Praying for justice, or vindication, is in fact the reason for
Jesus telling the parable in the first place (v. 1). Jesus, in this
parable and the one about the friend who came at midnight
(Luke 11:5–13), encourages people to pray until things change.
'The God of the Bible', says Walter Wink, 'invents history in
interaction with those who "hunger and thirst to see right
prevail." ' For 'history belongs to the intercessors, who believe
the future into being.'[44] This kind of prayer conquers fear, for
God is not like the judge, but is compassionate, and at work
in history.

In the Gospel of Luke, women and widows in particular are
identified as the *little ones*, or *those who cringe*, the poor. In
Palestinian society they counted for nothing. By using a widow
as the subject of the story, Jesus is declaring liberation for all
who are oppressed. When he offers her example of persistence
as a model for prayer, he is breaking yet another taboo, for
the prayers of women were not regarded as valid by the scribes
and Pharisees. By allowing the narrative to record the defeat
of the unjust judge, Jesus offers empowerment to all who are
treated unjustly, and offers the most marginalised in society as
an example.

It is from these unjustly treated and marginalised people
that Jesus obtains the answer to the question, 'when the Son
of man comes, will he find any faith on earth?' The answer is
yes, but in the unlikely persons of the outcast tax collector, like
Zacchaeus (19:9–10), and the widow.

Talking Points

'The God of the Bible', says Walter Wink, 'invents history in interaction with those who "hunger and thirst to see right prevail." ' He also says, 'History belongs to the intercessors, who believe the future into being.' Jesus, in the parable of the widow and the story of the friend who came at midnight (Luke 11:5–13), encourages people to make persistent prayer until things change. How can such insights change the way we pray, and for what we pray?

Reflection and Action

Intercession is both prayer and action. The unjust judge is defeated by the woman, not just because of her pleading, but because she knows what justice is, and that she is not receiving it. Her words, actions and petition are all part of her intercession. No wonder Jesus says it is among such people that faith will be found on the earth. What are the injustices about which you are concerned? How are you making intercession? How persistent are you? Look for solidarity in your group, and elsewhere, over some cause for which you need both prayer and action.

Worship

Follow the Liturgy for Justice on page 241.

For next week bring a candle and a holder from home; let this be a symbol for the cause upon which you have decided to intercede and act. Also choose a verse from the Bible that expresses your hope for justice in your chosen cause. Write a brief prayer. In your worship next time read your verse, and leave it with the group Focus (see p. 40). Make your prayer and light your candle, concluding as follows:

THE PERSON OFFERING PRAYER SAYS: Will not God see justice
                                     done if his chosen people
                                     pray day and night?

ALL RESPOND SAYING: I promise you that God
                                       will see justice done to
                                       them and with haste.

Take your candle home and light it as a reminder of your
prayer, and the prayers of others.

Pentecost 22

Getting started:
What is the greatest risk, or most difficult choice, you have
made in your life? Why?

Read Luke 16:1–9.
(Other readings: Deuteronomy 11:18–28; 1 John 2:22-end.)

1   He also said to his disciples, 'There was a rich man and he
    had a steward who was denounced to him for being wasteful
2   with his property. He called for the man and said, "What is
    this I hear about you? Draw me up an account of your
    stewardship because you are not to be my steward any
3   longer." Then the steward said to himself, "Now that my
    master is taking the stewardship from me, what am I to do?
    Dig? I am not strong enough. Go begging? I should be too
4   ashamed. Ah, I know what I will do to make sure that when
    I am dismissed from office there will be some to welcome me
    into their homes."
5   'Then he called his master's debtors one by one. To the
6   first he said, "How much do you owe my master?" "One
    hundred measures of oil," he said. The steward said, "Here,
7   take your bond; sit down and quickly write fifty." To another
    he said, "And you, sir, how much do you owe?" "One hundred
    measures of wheat," he said. The steward said, "Here, take
    your bond and write eighty."
8   'The master praised the dishonest steward for his astute-
    ness. For the children of this world are more astute in dealing
    with their own kind than are the children of light.

9   'And so I tell you this: use money, tainted as it is, to win
       you friends and thus make sure that when it fails you, they
       will welcome you into eternal dwellings.'

Comment

This is a story about compromise, expediency and taking risks.
The steward is responsible for his master's affairs and he has
been fiddling the accounts. In such cases he would be dismissed
and immediately imprisoned. Notice is served on the steward
(v. 2) who, by keeping silent, admits his guilt, but the news of
his dismissal is not yet in the public domain. By not being
thrown into jail, he has experienced mercy from his master.
He must now take the gamble that will, if it succeeds, prevent
him from having to 'dig' or 'beg' (v. 3).

The steward has just enough time to do a deal with his
master's debtors. If they discover his game, they will not play
along, so he has to act quickly, almost rudely (vv. 5–7). He
offers a straight reduction on their debt. By the time his master
gets to know the worst – that is, he has been deprived of even
more of his income, there will be people celebrating in the
village the most generous landlord of all time! And the steward
will be riding high too – for he is sure to have let the debtors
know that he has negotiated the deal.

The master is forced into a dilemma. If he exposes the
steward's action and demands the full dues, he would risk
the cursing and anger of the villagers. He has been revealed as
a generous man for not sending his steward to prison, and this
gamble has paid off. The steward has been saved and the master
has paid in full. The master 'praised the dishonest steward for
his astuteness' (v. 8) – or his skill at self-preservation! Of course
we do not know what happened to the steward, any more
than we know what happened to the older son in the parable
of the prodigal (Luke 15:11–30).

This story follows Jesus' command to his disciples to sell
surplus possessions (Luke 14:33). It also follows the stories
about losing and finding (Luke 15:1–30). The steward knows

that if the news gets about that he is sacked, then he will lose everything (v. 3). By finding a way of securing his own future, he is surprisingly commended by Jesus, who tells his disciples to learn from the ways of the world (vv. 8–9). 'Use money, tainted as it is, to win you friends.'

Having called his disciples to 'give up all they own' (12:32–4; 14:33), like him, for the sake of the 'lost' (15:1–3, 4–7, 10, 11–30), he warns them not to be like the 'Pharisees, who loved money' (16:14), but to make use of money, presumably made from the sale of surplus goods, to share with the poor. 'After all, says Jesus, God (the master) is a God of judgement and mercy. Because of his evil man (the steward) is caught in a crisis of the coming of the kingdom. The only option is to entrust *everything* to the unfailing mercy of a generous master who, he can be confident, will accept to pay the price for humanity's salvation.'[45]

Talking Points
Which people do you have admiration for, albeit grudging, who have an instinct for self-preservation?

Once again, in this parable Jesus returns to the issue of money. What do you think Jesus means when he says to the disciples, who have 'given up all they own', to 'use money, tainted as it is, to win you friends'? How much do we need money in the struggle for justice? How do we use it in the light of Jesus' assertion, 'You cannot be the slave of both God and money'? (Luke 16:13)

Worship
Offer the worship suggested last week.

For next time ask some members of the group to prepare a liturgy on the theme: *Planning for peace, a future and a hope.*

Reflection and Action
In the worship you have focused on a cause, or causes, about which you feel passionately. What other steps can you take to

persist in the struggle for justice in relation to your concern?
What part does money play? Are there 'surplus possessions'
you can sell, or persuade others to sell in the cause of right?

All of us, like the steward in the story, are caught in a 'crisis
of the coming kingdom'. We need to trust God for everything,
yet we empower God to act in his world through us. How will
you be consistent to both prayer and action?

Last Sunday after Pentecost

Getting started
What has been your most frustrating experience of waiting?
When has a time of waiting brought something worthwhile?

Read Jeremiah 29:1,4–14.
(Other readings: Philippians 3:7-end; John 17:1–10.)

1   **This is the text of the letter that the prophet Jeremiah sent
     from Jerusalem to those who were left of the elders in exile,
     to the priests, the prophets and all the people whom Nebuch-
     adnezzar had deported from Jerusalem to Babylon ...**

4   **'The Lord of hosts, the God of Israel, says this to all the
5   exiles deported from Jerusalem to Babylon: Build
6   houses, settle down; plant gardens and eat what they
     produce; marry and have sons and daughters; choose
     wives for your sons, find husbands for your daughters so
     that these can bear sons and daughters in their turn; you
7   must increase there and not decrease. Work for the good
     of the city to which I have exiled you; pray to the Lord
8   on its behalf, since on its welfare yours depends. For the
     Lord of hosts, the God of Israel, says this: Do not be
     deceived by the prophets who are with you or by your
9   diviners; do not listen to the dreams you have, since they
     prophesy lies to you in my name. I have not sent them,
10   the Lord declares. For the Lord says this: When the
     seventy years granted to Babylon are over, I shall inter-**

vene on your behalf and fulfil my favourable promise to
11   **you by bringing you back to this place. Yes, I know what**
    plans I have in mind for you, the Lord declares, plans
    for peace, not for disaster, to give you a future and a
12   **hope. When you call to me and come and pray to me, I**
13   **shall listen to you. When you search for me, you will find**
    me; when you search wholeheartedly for me, I shall let
14   **you find me (the Lord declares. I shall restore your**
    fortunes and gather you in from all the nations and
    wherever I have driven you, the Lord declares. I shall
    bring you back to the place from which I exiled you).'

Comment

The politics of expediency have failed. To the north, the emerging superpower empire of Babylon, to the south Egypt. Babylon feared trouble with Egypt and wanted to protect its borders. Babylon needed to control the Syrian-Palestinian corridor. Judah's king Jehoiakim wanted a non-aligned independent state of Judah. Jeremiah, a prophet called by God in the reign of Josiah (1:1), sees the futility of trying to form armies to defend such a state from the might of Nebuchadnezzar's war machine. He sees the effect on the poor of famine caused by siege and the requisitioning of crops for the invading armies. Day after day he acts out warnings to the leaders (ch. 28), but eventually the inevitable happens and the deportations begin (29:1).

Regarded by many as a subversive, even a traitor, he is arrested and buried alive in the hope he will recant (37:11–21; 38:1–6). As a prophet, Jeremiah was used to conflict. Much of his message held warnings of the impending conquest, but he is essentially a man of *hope*. To the first exiles he writes a letter encouraging them to accept the situation and to 'build houses, settle down, marry and have sons and daughters' (vv. 5–6). Exiles who revolt quickly become expendable, so Jeremiah encourages them to pray and 'work for the good of the city . . . since on its welfare you depend' (v. 7). He is not advocating acquiescence, but rather laying the plans for a new destiny which God will bring into being. 'When the seventy years granted to Babylon are over ... I will bring you back to the place from which I exiled you,' says God through the prophet (vv. 10, 14).

The hope is set out – the possibility of future generations returning from exile. Three tasks are identified for the exiles, marrying and producing children (v. 6), 'work for the good of the city' (v. 7) and prayer (vv. 7, 12, 13). The exiles are being invited into partnership with God. The prophet recognises that prayer is the means by which God mobilises energy and support for the fulfilling of his constant desire for all humanity to live to its full potential, in freedom, justice and peace. Jeremiah says to the exiles, 'Prayer that acknowledges the Powers becomes a form of social action. God's hands are effectively tied when we fail to pray. That is the dignity and urgency on our praying.'[46] The 'building and planting' in the city (v. 5) are in themselves a parable of what God has in mind for them (v. 11), 'plans for peace ... to give you a future and a hope' (v. 11).

Talking Points

Jeremiah was a reluctant prophet and activist! However, he did get used to conflict, and recognised the calling of God, both challenging the authorities of his time, but also supporting his fellow citizens forced into exile because of their policies. He gives practical advice to people in a hostile environment – 'work for the good of the city ... since on its welfare yours depends' (v. 7). What does such a challenge mean for us whose citizenship is of the Kingdom of God?

Reflection and Action

Once again the prophet reminds us that prayer is the means by which God mobilises energy and support to bring about freedom, justice and peace for all humanity. If God's hands are effectively tied when we fail to pray, what does that require of us as a group and a church?

How much do we want 'a future and a hope'? (v. 12) How much are we prepared to give for it?

Worship
Offer the worship suggested last week.

And finally! The final section of *Seeds of the Word* concludes with the **Ninth to Fifth Sundays before Christmas**. Decide what your plans are for meeting again as a group. Why not share a simple meal together soon and **celebrate** something of your life together?

BEFORE CHRISTMAS

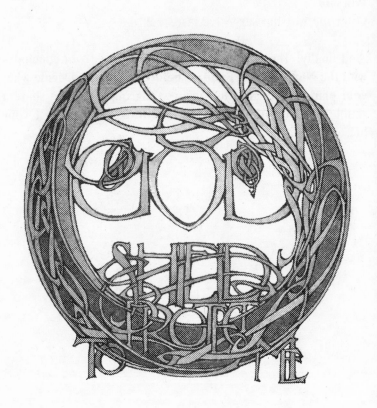

The Sundays before Christmas

Christmas comes earlier every year! When these Sundays begin, the Ninth to Fifth before Christmas, autumn is only just starting. The season of Advent, the four weeks before Christmas, provides an opportunity for preparing ourselves to celebrate the great feast. The purpose of Advent is to heighten our sense of expectation that Jesus is coming. So what is the purpose of weeks nine to five before Christmas?

During these weeks four big issues are addressed in the Sunday themes:

The Creation
The Fall
The Election of God's People
Preparing for God's Coming

Basic Preparation
As you begin *Seeds of the Word* for this time, don't forget to reread pages 23–7 to agree on the **why, where, and how** of your meeting, and to decide on responsibility for **ministries**.

The Liturgical Colour for this season is **green**.

Creating a Focus
Create a focus that reflects the theme of **creation**. In the northern hemisphere this is the autumn season; in the south the spring. Both provide many resources from nature: flowers, leaves, fruits, from which to make a focus.

Seasonal Collect:

> **Eternal God,**
> **We thank you for the glory of your creation –**
> **a mystery that surpasses our knowledge.**
> **Eternal God,**
> **We thank you for the earth, and**
> **water, sun and wind,**
> **creatures and peoples, cultures and nations:**
>
> **Guide us**
> **as we gather to confess**
> **that we have violated the gift of**
> **life given to us.**
>
> **Strengthen us**
> **as we seek to affirm that the earth and**

> **all therein is yours.**
> **Enable us**
> **as we seek to recall your**
> > **covenant and make it our own.'**

Use the **Seasonal Collect** to begin each meeting.

Note: These Sundays begin the Liturgical Year in *The Alternative Service Book 1980*. Nevertheless I have included them at the end of the book, because for most people in the Christian tradition the First Sunday in Advent marks the beginning of the Church's Year.

Ninth Sunday before Christmas

Getting started
Share with people in the group a contemplative moment when you have been moved, or touched by something beautiful in nature; or when something in another person has made you admire them for their courage or insight.

Read Genesis 1:1–3, 24–31; 2:1–3.
(Other readings: Colossians 1:15–20; John 1:1–14.)

1, 2 **In the beginning God created heaven and earth. • Now the earth was a formless void, there was darkness over the deep, with a divine wind sweeping over the waters.**

3   **God said, 'Let there be light,' and there was light.**

24   **God said, 'Let the earth produce every kind of living creature in its own species: cattle, creeping things and wild animals**

25   **of all kinds.' And so it was. God made wild animals in their own species, and cattle in theirs, and every creature that crawls along the earth in its own species. God saw that it was good.**

26   **God said, 'Let us make man in our own image, in the likeness of ourselves, and let them be masters of the fish of the sea, the birds of heaven, the cattle, all the wild animals**

and all the creatures that creep along the ground.'

27   God created man in the image of himself,
        in the image of God he created him,
        male and female he created them.

28 God blessed them, saying to them: 'Be fruitful, multiply, fill
    the earth and subdue it. Be masters of the fish of the sea, the
    birds of heaven and all the living creatures that move on
29 earth.' God also said, 'Look, to you I give all the seed-bearing
    plants everywhere on the surface of the earth, and all the
30 trees with seed-bearing fruit; this will be your food. And to
    all the wild animals, all the birds of heaven and all the living
    creatures that creep along the ground, I give all the foliage
31 of the plants as their food.' And so it was. God saw all he
    had made, and indeed it was very good. Evening came and
    morning came: the sixth day.
1   Thus heaven and earth were completed with all their array.
2   On the seventh day God had completed the work he had
    been doing. He rested on the seventh day after all the work
3   he had been doing. God blessed the seventh day, and made
    it holy because on that day he rested after all his work of
    creating.

Comment

This is a story about beginnings. It is about the beginning of
life and of God as the Source and Creator of life (vv. 1–3,
24–31). This account was probably written by priests who were
trying to re-found and re-establish the Jewish nation after fifty
or so years of exile in Babylon. This exile followed the downfall
of the monarchy. In this creation story women and men are
created equal and together in God's image (vv. 26–7). Those
returning from exile wanted to create a more equal society.
This story about all being equal in God's creative plan is written
to encourage the new community returning to rebuild their
nation. The God who creates also recreates (2:1–3). A community striving to rebuild needs periods of both work and rest,

in order to be blessed. To be blessed means to have a sense of
well-being, which is a gift of God. The seventh or 'sabbath'
day 'becomes a way of putting oneself in touch with and in
harmony with the way the universe operates.'[2]

The creation is seen as 'very good' (vv. 25, 31), and something
to be nurtured and stewarded by human beings (v. 28). God's
call to 'fill the earth and subdue it' (v. 28) has frequently been
mistakenly interpreted as an opportunity to exploit and pollute.
Today, people are increasingly aware of the fragility of the
planet and the balance of nature. Environmental awareness is
growing in people around the world, whether they practise
religion or not. There is an increasing recognition that the earth
should bring forth 'promises of good things, of fruitful lands,
of healthy children and wholesome living.'[3] Religion is about
the search for meaning. The writers of the Genesis story sought
to establish a new community founded on the belief that God
was both creator and the source of all good in human affairs.

A Chinese Christian writing about the hardships faced by
many peasants in his country commented,

> . . . but life is, as it has always been, also very precious
> and much loved. In hardships, suffering and struggle,
> people form relationships that have dimensions of the
> sacred. In revolutions they have sought justice, liberation,
> and human fulfilment for themselves. Even without refer-
> ence to an incarnator, life is and has been incarnate. With-
> out an ordainer, life is so ordained that the poor do rise
> up. Without any creation myth, creation is here and now.
> Life is down to earth, and revelation comes, if at all, from
> the very ground of suffering and hope.

What is religion in this setting? A possible answer is that it is
survival. 'It is the human struggle for life itself – its meaning,
purposes and destiny, even among tremendous and impossible
odds. Religion so defined is seen as an integral part of life
which is God given. It is not a *plus* to be appended to life.'[4]

Talking Points

Creation stories occur in many religions. The account in Genesis is part of the Jewish tradition which Christians have adopted. The story itself encourages good stewardship of the planet (vv. 27–9), yet so often human beings have exploited and destroyed. Environmental concerns have often been initiated by people who do not necessarily profess religious belief. Do you agree with the Chinese Christian who observed that religion for many people who struggle with life is *survival*? Is the purpose of Christian faith to 'seek justice' (Matthew 6:33) by re-helping the poor, working to promote peace, and encouraging care for our planet?

Reflection and Action

Is yours an 'environment-friendly' neighbourhood? In what ways? What needs improving? What can you as a group do to improve things? Are there people already seeking to make things better? Can you join with them? What role has a Christian community group in all this?

Worship

Read aloud the passage from Genesis. Keep a few moments of silence. Reflect on something which has moved or touched you; offer a short prayer beginning with the words: 'God saw all that was made, and it was very good, especially . . . (add group suggestions).'

Conclude with this prayer:

In the beginning God made the world.
Let us give thanks for all that God has made.

Think of a time when you saw the world is beautiful . . .
Think of a sunset over the hills,
or sunrise over a sleeping city.
Think of a running river,
or stars shining on a dark sea.

Think of a light flashing on a puddle,
or of geraniums growing in a window box.
Think of a time when you saw the world is beautiful –
and give thanks.

Think of a time when you found pleasure in your body.
Think of walking in the wind, or digging a garden.
Think of dancing till dawn, or climbing a mountain.

Think of giving birth to a child,
or of holding someone you love.
Think of a time when you found pleasure in your body
– and give thanks.[5]

Eighth Sunday before Christmas

Getting started
What has been the most shocking news story you have heard
this week? Why?

Read Genesis 4:1–10.
(Other readings: 1 John 3:9–13; Mark 7:14–23.)

1   **The man had intercourse with his wife Eve, and she conceived**
     and gave birth to Cain. 'I have acquired a man with the help
2   **of Yahweh,' she said. She gave birth to a second child, Abel,**
     the brother of Cain. Now Abel became a shepherd and kept
3   **flocks, while Cain tilled the soil. Time passed and Cain**
     brought some of the produce of the soil as an offering for
4   **the Lord, while Abel for his part brought the first-born of**
     his flock and some of their fat as well. The Lord looked with
5   **favour on Abel and his offering. But he did not look**
     with favour on Cain and his offering, and Cain was very angry
6   **and downcast. The Lord asked Cain, 'Why are you angry and**
7   **downcast? If you are doing right, surely you ought to hold**
     your head high! But if you are not doing right, Sin is crouching
8   **at the door hungry to get you. You can still master him.' Cain**

**said to his brother Abel, 'Let us go out'; and while they were
in the open country, Cain set on his brother Abel and killed
him.**

9   **The Lord asked Cain, 'Where is your brother Abel?' 'I do
not know,' he replied. 'Am I my brother's guardian?' 'What**
10   **have you done?' The Lord asked. 'Listen! Your brother's
blood is crying out to me from the ground.'**

Comment

This story is about the beginning of fratricide – brother killing
brother. A graphic and profoundly tragic story which carries
all the ingredients of human failing: greed, jealousy, ambition,
pride, lack of self-worth, envy, murder. That this is a story
intended to explain the age-old tragedy of human division is
indicated in the names of the chief players: Adam ('from the
ground') and Eve (to 'live'); Cain (a 'spear') and Abel (poss.
'breath, futility'). One is a farmer, the other a shepherd. The
two tasks are marked by different approaches to life (vv. 3–4).

Genesis is a retrospective book. We are not here dealing
with 'history as it happened', but rather with 'what happens
in history'. Different cults practise different rituals. Somehow
Abel's sacrifice of a sheep is 'looked on with favour' by God,
whereas Cain's harvest basket is rejected. There is no attempt
to explain why. (It *could* be that the fertility cults of the
Canaanites were so despised by the Hebrew priests that they
used this story to emphasise their abhorrence of such practices.)
Whatever the reason, Cain's sense of rejection leads him to
murder (v. 8).

At this point, the whole nature of the story changes. Cain
becomes a fugitive. Murder for whatever reason cannot be
justified or condoned. Although the answer 'Yes' is never given
explicitly to Cain's question, 'Am I my brother's guardian?' (v.
9), the whole tone of the punishment of 'a life of unrest and
harassment without peace' makes Cain see immediately that
'a life far from God is a life that God no longer protects.'[6] The
land of Nod means 'the place of the fugitive'. Banishment,

enforced exile, is a frightening prospect for tribal peoples whose lives depend on community. The story is meant to act as a warning for all time of the social consequences of murder. The source of the crime, in the spirit of the criminal, must be isolated so that it cannot spread further.

Talking Points

This story, like the account of creation in Genesis 1, is written by people seeking to re-establish community and nation. The question 'Am I my brother's guardian?' or 'Am I guardian to my kin?' is tacitly answered 'Yes'. Jesus asked a prior question, 'Who are my kin?' (Mark 3:33) and the lawyer asks in the story of the Samaritan, 'And who is my neighbour?' (Luke 10:29). Gender, race, class, poverty and wealth are all flash points in human relationships. Who are 'our kin'? Who is 'our neighbour'? What does it mean for us to be 'guardian to our kin'?

Reflection and Action

Report back on any action you may have taken since last time you met. What further action can you take?

Being guardian to our kin means firstly recognising who they are. Begin at work, 'recognise the diversity of class, race, gender backgrounds and economic status *among those we already associate with each day.*'[7] Watch for signs of prejudice and discrimination at work, in the neighbourhood, in church. Bring examples with you to your next meeting and discuss together how you might act in a positive way.

Worship

Be silent for a few moments. Reflect on the people or groups you have identified as 'kin'.

Someone should ask: 'Am I guardian to my kin?' All reply: 'I am guardian to my kin.' Someone else asks: 'Who is my neighbour? Who are my kin?' Taking it in turns, each should name someone or a group they have identified during the discussion. Conclude by having someone say, 'God says,

"Whom shall I send? Who will go for us?" ' All reply: 'Here I am. Send me.' Finish by saying the Lord's Prayer together.

Seventh Sunday before Christmas

Getting started
Share any insights you have had as a result of recognising who are your kin at work, at church, in the neighbourhood.

Read Genesis 12:1–9.
(Other readings: Romans 4:13-end; John 8:51-end.)

1   The Lord said to Abram, 'Leave your country, your kindred and your father's house for a country which I shall show
2   you; and I shall make you a great nation, I shall bless you and make your name famous; you are to be a blessing!

3   I shall bless those who bless you,
       and shall curse those who curse you,
       and all clans on earth
       will bless themselves by you.'

4   So Abram went as the Lord told him, and Lot went with him. Abram was seventy-five years old when he left Haran.
5   Abram took his wife Sarai, his nephew Lot, all the possessions they had amassed and the people they had acquired in Haran. They set off for the land of Canaan, and arrived there.
6   Abram passed through the country as far as the holy place at Shechem, the Oak of Moreh. The Canaanites were in the
7   country at the time. The Lord appeared to Abram and said, 'I shall give this country to your progeny.' And there, Abram
8   built an altar to the Lord who had appeared to him. From there he moved on to the mountainous district east of Bethel, where he pitched his tent, with Bethel to the west and Ai to the east. There he built an altar to the Lord and invoked the
9   name of the Lord. Then Abram made his way stage by stage to the Negeb.

Comment

This is a story of promise. It is the account of a promise given
to an old man (v. 4). Abraham, described as being 'as good as
dead' (Hebrews 11:12) is given a promise that God will 'bless'
ordinary human beings like Isaac, Jacob and Joseph, whose
family stories of births, marriages, migrations and death are
told in Genesis 12–50. These 'were a people who had their
roots outside the centres where the "important" people lived
and effective decision-making presumably took place.'[8] To
these people on the edge of society God gave the promise of
blessing (v. 3).

'Blessing' has different emphases in the Bible: sometimes it
is about receiving from God 'long life, increase of family, crops,
herds, peace and wealth';[9] at other times the emphasis is on
justice, righteousness and peace being bestowed on people who
are faithful to the command 'to do what is right, to love loyalty
and to walk humbly with your God' (Micah 6:8). The promise
to Abraham, Isaac, Jacob and others was not so much about
conquest or nationalism. Those who received blessing were
those ordinary people in whom God was keeping faith alive in
every generation. The blessing comes as people live together
in harmony. It is a promise that is always being fulfilled, but
which is still a long way from reaching everyone.

Many years ago I was given the words of a prayer, which I
wrote in my Bible: 'God, give us grace and vision to toil in the
field of time in the sense of the eternal.' It is a prayer for all
time, from Abraham to the present day. To receive the promise,
there has to be both a 'leaving' (v. 1) and a 'becoming' (v. 2).

Faith in the promise has to be passed on. Without faith in
the promise that God blesses humanity in every generation,
hope dies. Take a little time to read Hebrews 11 which provides
a detailed commentary on the people of faith who trusted the
promise, yet did not see it fulfilled. Like us, many of those
people were unworthy, fragile human beings, easily distracted
by personal ambition, greed, cowardice, sexual infidelity, and
yet capable in many instances of great courage:

Some had to bear being pilloried and flogged, or even chained up in prison. They were stoned, or sawn in half, or killed by the sword; they were homeless, and wore only the skins of sheep and goats; they were in want, hardship and maltreated ... These all won acknowledgement through their faith, but they did not receive what was promised ... they were not to receive perfection except with us. (Hebrews 11:36–40)

Talking Points

Whom can you identify as people who have attempted to keep the faith alive in our time? Why do we need God to be with us? What signs have you seen that God is 'blessing' today? We need God to be with us, because if and 'when we are robbed of past and future, set in timelessness, robbed of God and neighbour, there is only "I" remaining. Then life becomes short, empty and barbarous.'[10] Do you agree?

How can we hold on to the promise of 'a time yet to be', when oppression is overcome by liberation, the bereaved are comforted and orphans cared for? How do we cope with attacks that inevitably come when such an agenda is striven for?

Reflection and Action

'We have little sense of community with our five billion neighbours, scant knowledge of a harmonious relationship with the eco-system and, at root, little meaningful experience of our identity as the children of God. Our deep need is to find a way to connect. The broken relationships must be healed; everything now depends upon our making connections.'[11] What connections do you need to make in your neighbourhood, or community? What relationships need healing? Plan some initial steps to making connections and bringing healing.

Worship
Say together the prayer: 'God, give us vision to toil in the field
of time in the sense of the eternal.' Read the verses
from Hebrews 11:36–40. Keep silence and reflect on people
you have heard of, or know, who have kept faith in the midst
of great difficulty. After a few moments go round the group
simply mentioning their names. Conclude by holding hands
and saying: 'The grace of our Lord Jesus Christ, and the
love of God and the fellowship of the Holy Spirit be with
us.'

For next week prepare a short litany with the response: 'Let
my people go.' See if you can find a tape of the Afro-American
spiritual 'Go down Moses', or some other Freedom song. Also
try and locate Martin Luther's 'I have a dream' speech, and
have someone read it aloud to the group.[12]

Sixth Sunday before Christmas

Getting started
Share with your group an experience of healing in your life.
You might speak of healing from illness, a broken relationship,
or some emotional hurt. Take time to listen to each other.
Respect each other's confidence.

Read Exodus 3:7–15.
(Other readings: Hebrews 3:1–6; John 6:25–35.)

7   The Lord then said, 'I have indeed seen the misery of my
     people in Egypt. I have heard them crying for help on account
     of their taskmasters. Yes, I am well aware of their sufferings.
8   And I have come down to rescue them from the clutches of
     the Egyptians and bring them up out of that country rich and
     broad, to a country flowing with milk and honey, to the home
     of the Canaanites, the Hittites, the Amorites, the Perizzites,
9   the Hivites and the Jebusites. Yes indeed, the Israelites' cry
     for help has reached me, and I have also seen the cruel way
10   in which the Egyptians are oppressing them. So now I am

sending you to Pharaoh, for you to bring my people the Israelites out of Egypt.'

11   **Moses said to God, 'Who am I to go to Pharaoh and bring**
12   **the Israelites out of Egypt?' 'I shall be with you,' God said, 'and this is the sign by which you will know that I was the one who sent you. After you have led the people out of Egypt, you will worship God on this mountain.'**

13   **Moses then said to God, 'Look, if I go to the Israelites and say to them, "The God of your ancestors has sent me to you," and they say to me, "What is his name?" what am I**
14   **to tell them?' God said to Moses, 'I am he who is.' And he said, 'This is what you are to say to the Israelites, "I am has**
15   **sent me to you." ' God further said to Moses, 'You are to tell the Israelites, "Yahweh, the God of your ancestors, the God of Abraham, the God of Isaac and the God of Jacob, has sent me to you." This is my name for all time, and thus I am to be invoked for all generations to come.'**

Comment

This is a story of people 'who were at the very bottom of Egyptian society, effectively non-persons in the greatest empire of the day.' It is also the story of a God who takes sides (vv. 7–8); who offers hope and the concrete possibilities of a new home and opportunities to live in freedom. God is revealed 'as a God of the people, a God who stands by them when they are oppressed and exploited, a God of the poor who acts on behalf of the poor and the powerless to liberate and free them from slavery.'[13]

God makes a promise to 'come down to rescue' the Israelites (v. 8). He picks out Moses and says, 'So now I am sending you to Pharaoh, for you to bring my people the Israelites out of Egypt' (v. 10). Egypt's influence as a world power was significant at the time of the Israelites' captivity and enslavement. Moses was being challenged to face Pharaoh, to confront the power of empire he represented, and demand that it stop oppressing God's people. Moses knew that proposing the release of a slave force essential to the economic well-being of the country would meet implacable opposition (Exodus 4–12).

Liberating a demoralised and brutalised people (2:23) required vision and courage. The God of freedom (v. 8) is just and compassionate (vv. 7,9). Moses, the agent of that freedom, is to participate in dismantling 'the politics of oppression and exploitation by countering it with a *politics of justice and compassion*.'[14] The God of freedom is to be revealed to the captives by the simple device of story: the story of their *free* ancestors, Abraham, Isaac and Jacob. There can be no 'politics of justice and compassion unless we have a religion of God's freedom.' The reticence with which Moses faced the task is understandable: both he and his people were being asked to imagine the unimaginable: freedom and the demise of the system of oppression. The struggle would be long and hard. 'The point that prophetic imagination must ponder is that there is no freedom of God without the politics of justice and compassion, and there is no politics of justice and compassion without a religion of the freedom of God.'

Talking Points

Many people who experience oppression in our day and age have found the book of Exodus a symbol of hope in their struggle. People who are the 'bottom of the pile' socially and economically discover that God does not just save souls, but is actively struggling with them for justice, seeking to liberate them from their oppression. How do you react to such a view of God?

Many Christian groups in recent years have sought to put faith into action.

A new faith community has emerged in urban centres, homeless shelters, and soup kitchens; in street protests and jail cells; on racial and ecological battlegrounds; in prayer and bible study groups; and in diverse experiments in community and spiritual renewal. What has often been expressed as 'prophetic protest' now has the capacity to be a vital source of 'prophetic vision' as well. Out of religious values and moral concerns, new social and economic alternatives are emerging.[15]

What examples of 'prophetic protest' or 'prophetic vision' do you know about? What message are they giving to Church and nation?

Reflection and Action

How far have you got in identifying the connections you need to make in your neighbourhood, and the relationships that need healing? What examples of 'protest' and 'vision' can you see in your neighbourhood? What involvement have members of the group in these situations? Who holds the power?

During the next few weeks, plan to visit people who are 'taking sides' in your locality. Who needs empowering? Who needs their power challenged? Is God calling you, like Moses, to act? How?

Worship

Next week share a meal together. Ask each person to bring something easily prepared and simple. Invite someone to prepare a grace. The Fifth Sunday before Christmas is called 'Stir-up Sunday' and people often began to make their Christmas cake or pudding mix on this day, inviting all to stir the rich contents. Someone might like to bring their ingredients for all to stir! Conclude your meal and worship by saying together the Collect for the day:

> Stir up, O Lord,
> the wills of your faithful people;
> that, richly bearing the fruit of good works,
> they may by you be richly rewarded;
> through Jesus Christ our Lord.[16]

Fifth Sunday before Christmas

Getting started
Share your meal and offer your worship as suggested last week.

Read Matthew 24:37–44.
(Other readings: 1 Kings 19:9–18; Romans 11:13–24.)

37 'As it was in Noah's day, so will it be when the Son of man
38 comes. For in those days before the Flood people were eating,
       drinking, taking wives, taking husbands, right up to the day
39 Noah went into the ark, and they suspected nothing till the
       Flood came and swept them all away. This is what it will be
40 like when the Son of man comes. Then of two men in the
41 fields, one is taken, one left; of two women grinding at
       the mill, one is taken, one left.

42   'So stay awake, because you do not know the day when
43 your master is coming. You may be quite sure of this, that if
       the householder had known at what time of the night the
       burglar would come, he would have stayed awake and would
       not have allowed anyone to break through the wall of his
44 house. Therefore, you too must stand ready because the Son
       of man is coming at an hour you do not expect.'

Comment

'Where is he?' This was the question Christians faced in the
early days of the Church, because they believed that Jesus
would return to earth soon. In preparation for this, some
Christians chose to sell their possessions and live simply (Acts
2:44–5), and they prayed, shared common meals, and were
enthusiastic for learning the faith (Acts 2:42). Some even
decided not to get married, because 'the end was nigh' (1
Corinthians 7:26, 31). *However*, when Jesus didn't show up,
people began to get tired of radical living: conflicts broke
out, some people left the church, others betrayed one another
(10:35–7; 24:10); a few were led astray by false prophets
(24:4–5,11). 'A sense of the power of evil became strong (24:12).

With the power of evil increasing . . . a disregard for law and authority set in (24:12; 7:23; 13:41; 23:28).' Because such forms of 'wickedness' seemed to be multiplying, the love of 'most' in Matthew's households of faith was growing cold (24:10–12). 'Churches seemed to be following the normal social tendency of a religious movement to adapt gradually to the society around it.'[17]

Politically, events were moving fast. Around the time when Matthew's Gospel was published (70 CE) the Temple in Jerusalem was destroyed. Many Jewish Christians who would have had allegiance to the Temple in Jerusalem made pilgrimages. The sacking of the city and Temple added to people's fear, disillusionment and sense of panic. Matthew sought to allay these fears by recalling Jesus saying, 'Take care no one deceives you' and 'see that you are not alarmed' (24:4,6).

Many Christians, like people of all religions, tended to the view that Jesus could only be near them in special places, times or events. When war came many felt bereft. In the early part of his Gospel Matthew reminds Christians that Jesus is Emmanuel – *God with us* – and at the end of Jesus' promise, 'And look, I am with you always' (28:20). Jesus' presence is not limited by time, space, events or place.

In every generation Christian communities face the same temptations as those that beset Matthew's house churches. As with those ordinary, confused, frequently disillusioned, fearful and anxious people,

> Jesus is before us today, in the history we are living, a history whose scenarios are not all that different from his . . . After every step – every advance or defeat – there is another, new step to take, for this God claimed by Jesus of Nazareth is and has been the God of the living ever since Abraham, down through the entire history of the people of Israel and of humanity itself.[18]

Next week marks the beginning of Advent, a time of waiting,

preparing for the coming of the domination-free order of God – the just and gentle rule of the Kingdom.

Talking Points

In our generation we have witnessed many momentous events: the end of segregation in the United States; the dismantling of the Berlin Wall; the release of Nelson Mandela and his inauguration as president of one of the most racist countries in the world. Each of these events began with small movements of resistance and opposition. Eventually, the inexorable need and desire for justice has broken through once implacable opposition. It is no time to be complacent. Each of these events has the potential for creating new oppression; poverty, racism, sexism, prejudice, class divisions, environmental and ecological abuse still threaten to engulf humanity. 'Keep awake', declared Jesus. 'Be alert ... Let no one deceive you'. Where is the need for you as a group to 'keep awake'? What challenges do you face?

Reflection and Action

How are the plans going to visit people who are 'taking sides' in your locality? Whom have you identified as needing empowering? How are you seeking to act in solidarity?

As you prepare for **Advent**, decide together what you want from your group and your life together. *Seeds of the Word* for Advent begins on page 45.

PART 3

Resourcing
Seeds of the Word

RESOURCING *SEEDS OF THE WORD*

Seeds of the Word is a workbook, rather than a handbook. In the last two sections of the book there are some resources which will hopefully enhance community formation and biblical reflection.

In the **Resources for Worship** there are three liturgies which groups may find helpful particularly at an early stage in their development. The liturgies are for:

Advent
Peace and Reconciliation
Justice

In **Resources for Study** there is a recommended selection of books on:

The Bible
Creating Small Church Communities
Social Analysis
Worship

RESOURCES FOR WORSHIP

A Liturgy for Advent

Create an Advent wreath as the focus of your prayer. All that
is needed is five candles; four red or blue, and one white, one
for each week of Advent, and a fifth – usually in the centre –
to mark the coming of the Christ.

Begin in darkness and silence.

Light the candle.

Each week say:

> A candle light is a protest at midnight.
> It is non conformist.
> It says to the darkness,
> 'I beg to differ.'
>
> (Samuel Rayan)

You may also say:

> Today we remember the coming of God.
> The light shines in the darkness.
> May our gathering at this season
> Be a sign of hope and solidarity with the poor.

Throughout Advent use the Collect on page 46.

Song:

> Kindle a flame to lighten the dark
> and take all fear away.[1]

Reflection:
Someone reads,

> Advent
> A time to take stock
> A time to listen
> A time to learn
> A time to look forward
> A time of change.[2]

Let each person in the group make a simple reflection on one of the above statements saying something like: 'This Advent I want to make time to take stock (or listen, learn, look forward etc.) . . . in my life.' People may of course reflect on more than one concern.

When all have finished, keep a few moments' silence.
Say together:

> Grant us your light, O Lord,
> that the darkness of our hearts being done away
> we may be brought at the last
> to the light which is Christ.
>
> Jesus Christ is the Light of the world,
> **a light no darkness can quench.**[3]

A Liturgy for Peace and Reconciliation

Create a focus by making a small circle of stones or pieces of broken brick. Place inside the circle a tall candle, and a small night-light candle for each member of the group.

Begin in darkness and silence.

Light the candles and say:

> We light this candle for peace, Lord.
> May its light scatter the darkness;
> may its flame be a symbol of hope;

may its burning be a sign of faith
joining with many other lights for peace.
We light this candle for peace.
May our lives be an expression of peacemaking;
may we seek to be lights in a dark world,
pointing to you, Jesus, the Prince of Peace,
and following you in the way of peace.
Let the candle burn, as a sign for peace,
offered to you.[4]

Reflection

Reconciliation becomes more of an attitude than an
acquired skill; it becomes a stance assumed before a
broken world rather than a tool to repair that world ...
Reconciliation involves a fundamental repair to human
lives, especially to the lives of those who have suffered ...
That repair takes time – time that can make the participants feel insecure, but necessary time nevertheless for
beginning a new life.[5]

Take a few moments to reflect on the areas where reconciliation
is called for in:

your own life,
your community,
between nations.

You may wish to share with other people in your group these
areas for reconciliation, and ask for the prayers and support
of the group as you venture into acts of reconciliation. Say
together:

Confront us, O Christ, with the hidden prejudices and
fears which deny and betray our prayers. Enable us to see
the causes of strife. Remove from us all false sense of
superiority. Teach us to grow in unity with all God's
children. Amen.[6]

Song

> Within our darkest night,
> you kindle a fire that never dies away,
> that never dies away. (Taizé)

As you sing this Taizé chant, let each person in turn remove their candle from inside the circle of stones and bricks to the outside, symbolically breaking down the walls of division, and making reconciliation.

Close with sharing the **peace**:

> Christ is our peace, he has reconciled us to God in one body by the cross. We meet in his name and we share in his peace.

A Liturgy for Justice

Create a focus by placing a candle inside a small roll of barbed or razor wire. You might want to add other symbols of oppression and hope, such as a few links of chain, or a single flower in a vase.

Begin in silence.

Light the candle and say:

> Let justice flow like water,
> and uprightness like a never-failing stream!
> (Amos 5:24)

A confession

Let different people take turns around the group to read the biddings, and all join in in **God, forgive us:**

> For our incapacity to feel the sufferings of others,
> and our tendency to live comfortably with injustice,
> **God, forgive us.**

> For the self-righteousness which denies guilt,
> and the self-interest which strangles compassion,

God, forgive us.

For those who live their lives in careless unconcern,
who cry, 'Peace, peace' when there is no peace,
God, forgive us.

For our failings in community,
our lack of understanding,
God, forgive us.

For our lack of forgiveness, openness, sensitivity,
God, forgive us.

For the times when we are too eager to be better than
others,
when we are too rushed to care,
when we are too tired to bother,
when we don't really listen,
when we are too quick to act from motives other than
love,
God, forgive us.[7]

Read Luke 18:1–8. Offer short prayers for justice concluding
each one: God will see justice done.

Conclude with the **peace**:

Cease doing evil. Learn to do good,
search for justice – and the peace of God be with you.
And also with you.

RESOURCES FOR STUDY

What follows is neither exhaustive, nor without bias, but as I am always being asked 'What can I read?' or 'Where did that insight into the gospel come from?', the least I can do is offer the sources from which I've been nurtured.

The Bible

'Authority,' remarks Ched Myers, 'is nothing more nor less than how we read the Bible, and what we do with what we read. Authority is also interpretation and practice'. I agree as to sources; there is no substitute for the Bible itself, but the selection that follows has helped light the path.

The Old Testament

Bruggemann, Walter, *The Prophetic Imagination* (Fortress Press, 1978).

Praying the Psalms (St Mary's Press, 1980).

Hopeful Imagination (Fortress Press, 1986).

The Creative Word (Fortress, 1982).

Abiding Astonishment, Psalms, Modernity and the Making of History (Westminster, 1991).

The Bible and Post Modern Imagination (SCM, 1993).

Ceresko, Anthony R., *Introduction to the Old Testament – A liberation perspective* (Orbis/Geoffrey Chapman, 1992).

Gottwald, Norman K. (ed.), *The Bible and Liberation – Political and Social Hermeneutics* (Orbis, 1983).

Pleins, J. David, *The Psalms* (Orbis, 1993).

Vroon Rienstra, Marchiene, *Swallows' Nest* (Eerdmans and Gracewing).

The New Testament

Aukerman, Dale, *Reckoning with Apocalypse, Terminal Politics and Christian Hope* (Crossroad, 1993).

Bailey, Kenneth E., *Poet and Peasant and Through Peasant Eyes – A*

Literary Cultural Approach to the Parables in Luke (Eerdmans, 1988).

Cassidy, Richard J., *Jesus, Politics and Society, A Study of Luke's Gospel* (Orbis, 1978).

Society and Politics in the Acts of the Apostles (Orbis, 1987).

John's Gospel in New Perspective (Orbis, 1992).

Crosby, Michael H., *House of Disciples – Church, Economics and Justice in Matthew* (Orbis, 1988).

Cwiekowski, Frederick J., *The Beginnings of the Church* (Gill and Macmillan, 1988).

Elliott, Neil, *Liberating Paul, the Justice of God and the Politics of the Apostle* (Orbis, 1994).

Fror, Hans, *You Wretched Corinthians* (SCM Press, 1995).

Goulder, Michael, *A Tale of Two Missions* (SCM Press, 1994).

Howard-Brook, Wes, *Becoming the Children of God, John's Gospel and Radical Discipleship* (Orbis, 1994).

Kinukawa, Hisako, *Women and Jesus in Mark – a Japanese Feminist Perspective* (Orbis, 1994).

Lapide, Pinchas, *The Sermon on the Mount – Utopia or Program for Action?* (Orbis, 1986).

La Verdière, *Dining in the Kingdom of God: The origins of the Eucharist according to Luke* (Liturgy Training Publications, 1994).

Massyngbaerde Ford, J., *My Enemy is my Guest: Jesus and Violence in Luke* (Orbis, 1984).

Mesters, Carlos, *God, Where Are You? Rediscovering the Bible* (Orbis, 1995).

Myers, Ched, *Binding the Strong Man – a Political Reading of the Gospel of Mark's Story of Jesus* (Orbis, 1988).

Pallares, José Cardenas, *A Poor Man Called Jesus, Reflections on the Gospel of Mark* (Orbis, 1986).

Rensberger, David, *Overcoming the World, Politics and Community in John* (SPCK, 1989).

Richard, Pablo, *Apocalypse: A People's Common Book of Revelation* (Orbis, 1995).

Swartley, William M., *Mark: The Way for all Nations* (Herald Press, 1979).

Theissen, Gerd, *The Shadow of the Galilean* (SCM, 1987).

Yoder, John Howard, *The Politics of Jesus* (Eerdmans, 1972).

Creating Small Church Communities

Barreiro, Alvaro, *Base Ecclesial Communities* (Orbis, 1982).

Boff, Leonardo, *Ecclesiogenesis – The base communities re-invent the Church* (Collins Flame, 1986).

Eagleson and Torres (eds.), *The Challenge of Basic Christian Communities* (Orbis, 1981).

Fraser, Ian, *Re-inventing Theology* (Wild Goose Publications, 1980).
Living a Countersign (Wild Goose Publications, 1990).

Galdamez, Pablo, *Faith of a People – The Life of a Basic Christian Community in El Salvador* (Orbis/Dove/CIIR, 1986).

Hebblethwaite, Margaret, *Basic is Beautiful* (Fount, 1991).
Base Communities – An Introduction (Geoffrey Chapman, 1993).

Hinton, Jeanne, *Communities* (Eagle, 1993).
Walking in the Same Direction – A New Way of Being Church (WCC/Risk, 1995).

Hoornaert, Eduardo, *The Memory of the Christian People* (Burns and Oates, 1989).

Marins, José, Carolee Chanona and Teo Trevisan, *The Church from the Roots* (CAFOD, 1990).

Myers, Ched, *Who Will Roll Away the Stone? Discipleship Queries for First World Christians* (Orbis, 1994).

O'Halloran, James, *Signs of Hope – Developing Small Christian Communities* (Orbis, 1991).
Living Cells (Dominican/Orbis).
Small Christian Communities – A Pastoral Companion (Orbis/Columba Press, 1996).

Winter, Derek, *Communities of Freedom* (Christian Aid, 1988).

Veling, Terry, *Living in the Margins – Intentional Communities and the Art of Interpretation* (Crossroad/Harder 1996).

Social Analysis

Arbuckle, Gerald A., *Earthing the Gospel – Inculturation Handbook for Pastoral Workers* (Geoffrey Chapman/Orbis, 1990).

Brown, Robert McAfee, *Unexpected News – Reading the Bible with Third World Eyes* (Westminster Press, 1984).

Earley and McKenna, *Actions Speak Louder – A Source Book for Social Ministry* (Columba, 1987).

Healy and Reynolds, *Social Analysis in the Light of the Gospel* (Columba, 1983).

Holland and Henriot, *Social Analysis Linking Faith and Justice*, (Orbis, 1991).

Mesters, Carlos, *Defenceless Flower* (Orbis/CIIR).

Wink, Walter, *Transforming Bible Study, a Leader's Guide* (Mowbray, 1990).

The Bible in Human Transformation (Fortress/SCM, 1993).

Naming the Powers; *Unmasking the Powers*; *Engaging the Powers* (Fortress Press, 1994).

Wylie-Kellermann, Bill, *Seasons of Faith and Conscience – Kairos, Confession Liturgy* (Orbis, 1991).

Worship

Bell, John L. and Graham Maule, *Wild Goose Songs* (Wild Goose Publications, Iona Community).

Bread of Tomorrow – Praying with the World's Poor, edited by Janet Morley (SPCK, Christian Aid, 1992).

Celebration–Reflections from the World Church, compiled by David Pain and Wendy Robins (USPG, 1992).

Celtic Daily Prayer, A Northumbrian Office (Marshall Pickering, 1994).

Dare to Dream, a Prayer and Worship Anthology from Around the World, edited by Geoffrey Duncan (Fount, 1995).

Let All the World: Liturgies, Litanies and Prayers from Around the World, edited by Wendy Robins (USPG, 1990).

Morley, Janet, *All Desires Known* (SPCK, 1992).

O'Malley, William J., SJ, *Daily Prayers for Busy People* (St Mary's Press).

The Alternative Service Book 1980 (Clowes, SPCK).

The Iona Community Worship Book (Wild Goose Publications, 1988).

The Promise of His Glory – Services and Prayers for the Season from All Saints to Candlemas (Mowbray/Church House, 1991).

The SPCK Book of Christian Prayer (SPCK, 1995).

Various Volumes of Music and Songs:

Caorineadh na Maighdine, Noiron ni Riain (Gaelic Music).

Music from Taizé Volumes 1–3 (Collins).

Tapes from Taizé: *Laudate – Music of Taizé; Cantate! Canons et Litanies*; *Resurrexit*.

World Praise Volumes 1 and 2, compiled by Geoff Weaver (Marshall Pickering, 1995).

Programmes and Courses

New Way of being Church. Weekend courses to encourage the development of small Christian communities, held at the College of the Ascension, Weoley Park Road, Selly Oak, Birmingham B29 6RD. Details from the Administrator.

USPG (The United Society for the Propagation of the Gospel) has Short-term Experience Programmes in the United Kingdom and overseas. In the UK this programme is known as *Root Groups* and provides opportunities for young people between 18–30 to live and work together in small communities for up to one year. Details from the STEP Personnel Officer, USPG, Partnership House, 157 Waterloo Road, London SE1 8XA.

NOTES

Preface

1. Marcel Moring, *The Great Longing* (Flamingo, 1995).

Chapter 1

1. Aho Byung Mu, 'Jesus and the Minjung in the Gospel of Mark' in *Minjung Theology – People as Subjects of History* (Orbis).
2. Marins, Chanona, Trevisan, 'The Church in Latin America', in *Trends in Mission towards the Third Millenium, Essays in Celebration of Twenty-five Years of SEDOS*, edited by William Jenkinson and Helena O'Sullivan (Orbis, 1991).

Chapter 2

1. Sean Fagan, 'The Vocation and Mission of the Laity', in *Trends in Mission towards the Third Millenium*, edited by William Jenkinson and Helena O'Sullivan (Orbis, 1991).
2. C. Earley and G. McKenna, *Actions Speak Louder Than Words* (Columba, 1987).
3. Carlos Mesters, 'The Bible in Christian Communities' in *The Challenge of Basic Christian Communities*, edited by Sergio Torres and John Eagleson (Orbis, 1981).

Chapter 3

1. Walter Wink, *Engaging the Powers* (Fortress Press, 1994).
2. Nikos Kazantzakis, *Report to Greco* (Faber and Faber, 1973).
3. Paul Simon, 'The Sound of Silence', CBS Records.
4. Adapted from Marcel Moring, *The Great Longing* (Flamingo, 1995).

Chapter 4

1. This story by Dee Price is abridged from an article 'A Candle in the Darkness' published in *Christian*, Winter 1993.
2. 'Prayer and the Powers', published in *Sojourners*, October 1990.
3. David Bosch, *Transforming Mission* (Orbis).

4. Walter Wink, *Engaging the Powers* (Fortress, 1995).

5. This and subsequent quotations are from Wink, op.cit.

6. Marcel Moring, *The Great Longing* (Flamingo, 1995).

7. *The SPCK Book of Christian Prayer* (SPCK, 1995).

8. Pierre Bockel, 'Malraux and the Challenge of Faith' in *Malraux, Life and Work*, edited by Martin de Courel, Weidenfield and Nicholson.

9. Robert Coles, *The Spirituality of Children* (Houghton Mifflin).

Chapter 5

1. Gilbert Cope, 'Colours Liturgical' in *A Dictionary of Liturgy and Worship*, edited by J.G. Davies (SCM Press).

2. Anthony de Mello, *The Song of the Bird* (Image).

Advent

1. *The Alternative Service Book 1980* (SPCK, Clowes), p. 422.

Epiphany

1. David Bosch, *Transforming Mission* (Orbis).

2. *The Alternative Service Book 1980*, p. 460.

3. Wes Howard-Brook, *Becoming the Children of God – John's Gospel and Radical Discipleship* (Orbis, 1994).

4. Eduardo Hoornaert, *The Memory of the Christian People* (Burns and Oates, 1989). My list of 'virtues' is adapted also from this book.

5. C.S. Lewis, *Mere Christianity* (Fontana). I am grateful to Mark Link in his *In the Stillness is the Dancing*, for the juxtaposition of the Hebrews' quote and that of C.S. Lewis.

6. *The Alternative Service Book 1980*, p. 486.

7. Pinchas Lapide, *The Sermon on the Mount – Utopia or Program for Action?* (Orbis, 1986), (parentheses mine).

8. Ibid., p. 27.

9. Ched Myers, *Binding the Strong Man – A Political Reading of the Gospel of Mark's Story of Jesus* (Orbis, 1988).

10. Ibid.

Lent

1. Bill Wylie-Kellerman, *Seasons of Faith and Conscience – Kairos, Confession, Liturgy* (Orbis, 1991).
2. Many people have difficulties with the language of 'King' and 'Kingdom'. I prefer Walter Wink's use of the term *God's Domination Free Order* (see Walter Wink, *Engaging the Powers*, Fortress Press, p. 107). He says that the terms 'kingdom' or 'reign' of God are altogether lacking in any gripping content and monarchical language is perceived as both sexist and androcratic ('rule by males'). Consequently, Jesus' vision of a new world in process of coming has been lost, even for most Christians.
3. *The Alternative Service Book 1980*, p. 499.
4. Walter Wink, op.cit.
5. Walter Wink, quoted by Bill Wylie-Kellermann, in an article entitled 'Spirits of the Age', published in *Sojourners*, May 1988.

Passiontide

1. David Rensberger, *Overcoming the World – Politics and Community in John* (SPCK, 1989).
2. Litany for Good Friday, taken from *Let All the World*, ed. Wendy S. Robins (USPG).
3. Bill Wylie-Kellermann, *Seasons of Faith and Conscience – Kairos Confession, Liturgy* (Orbis, 1991).
4. Ched Myers, *Binding the Strong Man* (Orbis, 1988).
5. Ibid., p. 389.
6. Ibid., p. 395 (words in parenthesis mine).
7. Ibid., pp. 396–7.
8. Ruben Alves, *All Year Round* (British Council of Churches).

Easter

1. Ched Myers, *Binding the Strong Man* (Orbis, 1988).
2. *The Alternative Service Book 1980*, p. 598.
3. Wes Howard-Brook, *Becoming the Children of God – John's Gospel and Radical Discipleship* (Orbis, 1994), p. 446.
4. Ibid., p. 448.
5. Ibid., p. 450.
6. Prayer by Robin Green, taken from *Celebration–Reflections from*

a World Church, edited and compiled by Wendy S. Robins and David Pain (USPG).

7. Howard-Brook, op.cit., p. 457.
8. Howard-Brook, op.cit., p. 457.
9. Robert McAfee Brown, *Unexpected News – Reading the Bible with Third World Eyes* (Westminster).
10. Howard-Brook, op.cit., pp. 467–8.
11. Howard-Brook, op.cit., p. 480.
12. Benedicta Ward, *Sayings of the Desert Fathers* (Mowbrays).
13. Walter Wink, *Engaging the Powers* (Fortress Press, 1994).
14. Howard-Brook, op.cit., p. 353.
15. Howard-Brook, op.cit., p. 357.

Ascension, Pentecost and Trinity

1. *The Alternative Service Book 1980*, pp. 627, 635, 640 respectively.
2. Ched Myers, *Binding the Strong Man* (Orbis).
3. Ibid.
4. Janet Morley, *All Desires Known* (SPCK, 1992).
5. Walter Wink, *Naming the Powers* (Fortress Press, 1994).
6. Ibid.
7. Quoted in Bill Wylie-Kellermann, *Seasons of Faith and Conscience – Kairos, Confession and Liturgy* (Orbis, 1991).
8. Alan Kreider, *Journey towards Holiness* (Marshall Pickering, 1987).

The Pentecost Season

1. Ulrich Schaffer, *Into Your Light* (IVP).
2. Wes Howard-Brook, *Becoming the Children of God – John's Gospel and Radical Discipleship* (Orbis, 1994).
3. Ibid.
4. Ibid.
5. Ibid., p. 395.
6. David Rensberger, *Overcoming the World – Politics and Community in John* (SPCK, 1989).
7. Richard J. Cassidy, *John's Gospel in New Perspective* (Orbis, 1992).
8. Howard-Brook, op.cit.
9. Eduardo Hoornaert, *The Memory of the Christian People* (Burns and Oates, 1989).

10. Wayne Meeks, *The First Urban Christians, The Social World of the Apostle Paul* (Yale University Press).

11. Ched Myers, *Who Will Roll Away the Stone? – Discipleship Queries for First World Christians* (Orbis).

12. Ibid.

13. Adapted from Ched Myers, op.cit.

14. Quotation from *Catholic Worker.*

15. *Hymns for Today's Church* (Hodder and Stoughton), no. 63.

16. All quotes in this section are from Kenneth E. Bailey, *Poet and Peasant and Through Peasant Eyes* (Eerdmans, 1988).

17. Michael H. Crosby, *House of Disciples, Church, Economics and Justice in Matthew* (Orbis, 1988).

18. John Howard Yoder, *The Politics of Jesus* (Eerdmans).

19. The address of Jubilee 2000 is: Christian Aid, PO Box 100, London, SE1 7RT.

20. Howard-Brook, op.cit.

21. Walter Wink, *Engaging the Powers* (Fortress, 1994).

22. Walter Wink, *Naming the Powers, Unmasking the Powers* and *Engaging* the Powers (Fortress).

23. Howard-Brook, op.cit.

24. Howard-Brook, op.cit.

25. Howard-Brook, op.cit., p. 369.

26. Howard-Brook, op.cit.

27. Hisako Kinukawa, *Women and Jesus in Mark – a Japanese Feminist Perspective* (Orbis, 1994).

28. Ibid., p. 132.

29. Wink, *Engaging the Powers.*

30. Robert Coles, *The Spiritual Life of Children* (Houghton Mifflin).

31. Ched Myers, *Binding the Strong Man* (Orbis, 1988).

32. Crosby, op.cit.

33. Philip Hallie, *Lest Innocent Blood Be Shed* (Michael Joseph).

34. G.V. Jones, *The Art and Truth of Parables* (London, 1964).

35. Bailey, op.cit.

36. Janet Morley, *All Desires Known* (SPCK, 1992).

37. J. Massynbaerde Ford, *My Enemy is my Guest – Jesus and Violence in Luke* (Orbis, 1994).

38. F.D. Bruner, *A Theology of the Holy Spirit* (Grand Rapids).

39. Pinchas Lapide, *The Sermon on the Mount – Utopia or Program for Action?* (Orbis, 1986).
40. Ibid.
41. Wink, *Engaging the Powers*. See my explanatory note (Lent, note 2).
42. Ibid.
43. Crosby, op.cit.
44. Wink, *Engaging the Powers*.
45. Bailey, op.cit.
46. Wink, *Engaging the Powers*, p. 317.

Before Christmas

1. Quoted in *Celebration–Reflections from a World Church* (USPG).
2. Anthony R. Ceresko, *Introduction to the Old Testament – A liberation perspective* (Orbis, 1992).
3. Matthew Fox, *Original Blessing* (Bear and Co.).
4. 'China Notes' by Franklin J. Woo in *The Bible and Liberation*, edited by Norman K. Gottwald (Orbis).
5. Quoted in *Celebration-Reflections from a World Church* (USPG), originally printed in *In the Beginning* (Wild Goose Publications).
6. Gerhard Von Rad, *Genesis* (SCM Press).
7. Ched Myers, *Who Will Roll Away the Stone? – Discipleship Queries for First World Christians* (Orbis, 1994). I have added 'gender, race and economic status'.
8. Ceresko, op.cit.
9. Alan Richardson, *A Theological Word Book of the Bible* (SCM Press).
10. Walter Bruggemann, *The Creative Word* (Fortress Press, 1982).
11. Jim Wallis, *Soul of Politics* (Fount).
12. This speech is in *Strength to Love*, Martin Luther King Jnr (Fortress Press).
13. Ceresko, op.cit.
14. The quotations in this section are from Walter Bruggemann, *The Prophetic Imagination* (Fortress Press, 1978).
15. Jim Wallis, *Soul of Politics* (Fount).
16. *The Alternative Service Book 1980*.
17. The quotations in this section are taken from Michael J. Crosby, *House of Disciples* (Orbis, 1988).

18. George Casalis, 'Methodology for a West European Theology of Liberation' in *Doing Theology in a Divided World*, edited by Fabella and Torres (Orbis).

Resources for Worship

1. *Wild Goose Songs*, vol. 1 (Wild Goose Publications, Iona Community).
2. *God Be With Us* (Christian Aid).
3. These prayers are from *The Promise of His Glory – Services and Prayers for the Season from All Saints to Candlemas* (Mowbray/ Church House Publishing).
4. John Johansen-Berg, *SPCK Book of Christian Prayer* (SPCK).
5. Robert Schreiter, *Reconciliation* (Orbis).
6. *Vancouver Assembly Worship Book* (WCC, 1983).
7. Pietermaritzburg Agency for Social Awareness, South Africa.